HUMAN RIGHTS AND
GLOBAL DIVERSITY

Books of Related Interest

FOUCAULT
Editor: Robert Nola, University of Auckland

PLURALISM AND LIBERAL NEUTRALITY
Editors: Richard Bellamy, Reading University and Martin Hollis,
University of East Anglia

FEMINISM, IDENTITY AND DIFFERENCE
Editor: Susan Hekman, University of Texas at Arlington

THE CHALLENGE TO FRIENDSHIP IN MODERNITY
Editors: Preston King, Lancaster University and Heather Devere,
Auckland Institute of Technology

THINKING PAST A PROBLEM
Preston King, Lancaster University

Human Rights and Global Diversity

Editors

SIMON CANEY and
PETER JONES

FRANK CASS
LONDON • PORTLAND, OR

First published in 2001 in Great Britain by
FRANK CASS PUBLISHERS
2 Park Square, Milton Park,
Abingdon, Oxon, OX14 4RN

and in the United States of America by
FRANK CASS PUBLISHERS
270 Madison Ave,
New York NY 10016

Transferred to Digital Printing 2005

Website: www.frankcass.com

Copyright © 2001 Frank Cass & Co. Ltd

British Library Cataloguing in Publication Data

Human rights and global diversity
1.Human rights 2. Globalization 3. Human rights – Public
opinion – Regional disparities
I. Caney, Simon II. Jones, Peter, 1945 –
323

ISBN 0 7146 5134 6 (cloth)
ISBN 0 7146 8161 X (paper)

Library of Congress Cataloging in Publication Data

Human rights and global diversity / editors, Simon Caney and Peter
Jones
    p.m
Include bibliographical references and index.
ISBN 0-7146-5134-6 (cloth) – ISBN 0-7146-8161-X (pbk.)
1. Human rights. 2. Human rights–Cross-cultural studies. 3. Cultural
relativism. 4. World citizenship. I. Caney, Simon. II. Jones, Peter,
1945-
JC571 .H768813 2001
323–dc21
                                                        00-011442

This group of studies first appeared in a Special Issue on 'Human Rights and Global
Diversity' of *Critical Review of International Social and Political Philosophy* 3/1
(Spring 2000) ISSN 1369-8230 published by Frank Cass.

Contents

1

Introduction

PETER JONES and SIMON CANEY

This collection of papers has its origins in a colloquium organised by the Centre for Political Thought at the University of Newcastle.[1] The colloquium reflected the growing interest of political philosophers in international issues and the growing interest of students of international politics in the ethical dimensions of their subject. The particular subject of the colloquium was the combination of two prominent concerns of contemporary international politics: the development of norms that are global in scope, and recognition and concern for the diversity of culture, belief and value to be found among humanity. In this brief introduction, we present an overview of the issues explored in the colloquium and in the papers that make up this collection.

The issue of how we should provide for populations characterised by a diversity of culture, belief and value has been a major preoccupation of contemporary political philosophy. For the most part, political philosophers have examined that issue as one that arises within states and that challenges states to find ways of providing for these diversities that can claim to be fair or just. If we go beyond the state and aspire to develop norms that are global in reach and application, we confront the issues posed by diversity in much more radical forms. Despite the multicultural character of many modern societies, humanity as a whole still exhibits a degree of cultural diversity that far outstrips that encapsulated within any particular state.

How then should we go about developing global norms in a context of global diversity? Can we simply take the various strategies that political philosophers have proposed for coping with intra-state diversity and transpose them to humanity as a whole? A transposition of that sort is implicit in the work of political philosophers who seek to move from the local to the global by extending concepts such as citizenship, that we normally associate with states, to humanity as a whole. Yet, as Chris Brown argues here, a simple extension of ideas from the domestic to the global may take too much for granted. In particular, he challenges the oft-made claim that we now have an emergent 'global civil society'. Pointing out the peculiar features of what is commonly called 'civil society' and the peculiar historical circumstances that gave rise to it within western societies, Brown argues that there exists nothing currently that we can properly call 'global civil society' and little reason to suppose that any such thing will develop in the foreseeable future. Such misapplied ideas, he suggests, do not merely misdescribe our world, they set us in pursuit of the wrong sort of global norms.

We may therefore be unrealistic about the current world, and misguided about its likely future, if we suppose that we can apply to it the categories and concepts that we associate with states and state membership. But perhaps we have no need to claim so much. Perhaps we can develop an adequate set of global norms without pretending that there is or ought to be a global community that is something like a macrocosmic version of the modern state. The idea of 'humanity' has been a powerful one for many centuries and probably has greater moral and political potency at the opening of the new millennium than at any previous historical moment. A conception of ourselves as fellow human beings may be all that we need to ground a set of global norms. It is that conception that has provided the foundation for the one of the most prominent transnational norms of our time: the idea of human rights. No other idea of global standards of conduct has secured such widespread recognition either in established international institutions or in the thinking of ordinary people.

Just because it has achieved such prominence, the idea of human rights has also been the global norm that has attracted most critical attention. In particular, the juxtaposition of human rights to cultural diversity has become the form in which the potential conflict between global norms and diverse cultures has been most commonly formulated. That putative conflict is often thought to require a simple choice between asserting human rights and respecting cultural difference. A doctrine of human rights that ignores the fact of cultural diversity and that brooks no compromise with it is certainly a possibility. Yet that has not generally been the spirit in which human rights have been espoused. While a doctrine of human rights must impose some limits upon what it finds acceptable, it can still take seriously people's diverse beliefs and commitments and strive to accommodate them.

How then might the idea of human rights reconcile itself with the fact of global diversity? Peter Jones and Simon Caney present different sorts of answer to that question. Jones proposes reconciliation through a theory of human rights that would seek to make these 'discontinuous' with, that is, essentially different in character from, other beliefs and values. In that theory, human rights would be grounded independently of the diverse beliefs and cultures to be found among humanity and would seek to regulate, rather than to compete with, that diversity. The merit of this approach is that it would enable the doctrine of human rights to accommodate cultural diversity without being compromised by it, but, for it to succeed, people would have to be persuaded to subordinate their most cherished cultural commitments to a regulatory doctrine of human rights.

The possible tension between the demands of human rights and the pull of cultural commitments could be avoided to the extent that rights and cultures have complementary rather than competing contents. A more happy marriage between the two might therefore be achieved in so far as there is 'continuity' rather than 'discontinuity' between human rights and the variety ethical traditions to be found among humanity. That is a possibility that Simon Caney explores. Rejecting the simple view that ethical traditions must be either for or against human rights, he shows how the two may exist in a variety of complementary relations and uses the example of Theravada Buddhism to make the case that the values commonly embodied in human rights are not uniquely western.

Caney also explores the question of why we should be concerned to reconcile human rights with diverse ethical traditions. He canvasses several reasons. One important consideration is that of securing uncoerced peace and harmony. Another stresses the importance of legitimacy; global norms will enjoy legitimacy only if they treat different cultures with respect and do not seek to repress them. On this view, we should respect a culture because we should respect those who bear it and for whom it has special significance. That in turn, however, raises the question of how we should conceive the 'bearers' that should be the objects of our respect. Within the human rights tradition, the individual person has been conceived as the primary bearer of entitlements. Yet there have also been many voices within that tradition that have insisted that fundamental rights can be borne by groups as well as by individuals. Since cultures are necessarily group phenomena, rights that people hold in respect of their cultures are among those that might be most plausibly conceived as group rights.

That is a view that Tom Hadden urges us to consider. He challenges a number of assumptions commonly made about human rights, including the assumption that they can be held only by individuals. Against that assumption, he suggests that several rights asserted within the human rights tradition are rights that can be held by individuals or by groups or by both, and shows how, during the past two centuries, rights associated with the claims of minorities and communities have swung, in a pendulum-like fashion, between rights ascribed to individuals and rights ascribed to groups. He also indicates the political nature of the choices that have to be made by drafters of statements of rights in striking an appropriate contextualised balance between individual claims and the claims of communities.

The tension between the claims of individuals and those of groups is also central to Kimberly Hutchings' essay. No group right has been asserted more frequently and with greater passion than the right of collective self-determination, and no international norm has entrenched itself more firmly in the international system than the right of national self-determination (in spite of, and perhaps partly because of, the ambiguities that afflict the adjective 'national'). But as soon as we invoke ideas of self-determination, we confront the issue of which of several possible 'selves' should be self-determining. If we ascribe the right of self-determination to more than one sort of 'self', we have to decide how we should deal with the potentially competing rights of those different selves. Hutchings examines how individual and collective forms of self-determination have been variously understood and idealised by liberal statists, liberal nationalists, communitarians, and civic republicans, and how those theorists have sought to reconcile ideals of individual and collective self-determination. She argues that the alternative approaches offered by critical theory, post-modernism and feminism present a better prospect than the more orthodox approaches of overcoming a simple polarity between the claims of individuals and those of collectivities.

Mark Bevir also presses the claims of post-structuralist thinking against those of liberal orthodoxies. He explains how Derrida traced Heidegger's Nazism to a metaphysic of spirit that led Heidegger to reify the German nation and to embrace a spiritual form of racism. For Derrida, the root of Heidegger's error lay in his metaphysical thinking and avoidance of that error should lead us to a cosmopolitan ethic, so that our recognition of difference and otherness will simultaneously entail an inclusive conception of humanity. That may seem to place Derrida in the same camp as the liberal universalist but, Bevir argues, Derrida's cosmopolitanism differs from liberalism in several fundamental respects. In particular, the metaphysical thinking that Derrida seeks to avoid and that led to Heidegger's error is still present, Bevir believes, within liberal thinking. In addition, Derrida's cosmopolitanism, rather than asserting a set of principles or rights, presents us with a different sort of ethic: a call to a practice of friendship toward others and to an openness and generous hospitality to their otherness.

Formulating norms is one thing; implementing them is another. Unsurprisingly, there has been a greater readiness among bodies such as the United Nations to propound global norms than to sanction their enforcement. Here again, there is an important disanalogy with the domestic case. The domestic government of a state is authorised to regulate relations between its citizens and to intervene when one of its citizens violates the rights of another. But no transnational body, including the United Nations, enjoys a parallel form of authority in the global case. Thus, when a state, or a coalition of states, intervenes to put right the wrongs of another state that is less akin to a government's wielding authority over its subordinates than to one or more private individuals intervening in a conflict between other private individuals. The relationship between the subjects and the objects of humanitarian intervention remains more horizontal than vertical in nature, and that makes intervention designed to uphold global norms a complex matter, both morally and pragmatically.

Nicholas Wheeler suggests three possible analogues to which states might conform when they engage in humanitarian intervention: the posse, the vigilante, and the norm entrepreneur. Using the case of NATO's intervention in Kosovo, he explores the extent to which current international law permits intervention for humanitarian reasons. The NATO powers claimed legal as well as moral justification for their intervention, but whether their action was actually sanctioned by international law is, Wheeler shows, very much open to question. In making their case, NATO's spokesmen and defenders pushed established law to its limits and arguably beyond its limits (as states such as Russia, China and India objected), extending, rather than merely observing, the boundaries of legally permissible intervention. Thus, Wheeler argues, while intervention in Kosovo conformed in part to the model of the vigilante, it also matched that of the 'norm entrepreneur', since NATO's defence of its action sought to persuade the international community to embrace new norms rather than merely to exercise established legal powers.

The case of humanitarian intervention illustrates well how the contingencies of international politics affect the form in which the ethical issues of international life confront us. In principle, the issue of humanitarian intervention has always been there, but, in practice, during the cold-war years the destabilising consequences that would have followed upon an international act of good Samaritanism made it effectively a non-option. With the end of the cold war, the risks to world peace involved in humanitarian intervention have significantly receded so that governments now have to face decisions about the scope of their responsibilities that they had previously been spared.

The same is true of the ethics of international affairs more generally. The idea of global norms is as old as the idea of natural law and most of the issues examined in this volume might, in principle, have been considered at any time during the past two millennia. But circumstances clearly do affect which issues we experience as pressing at any particular moment and which we do not. A world in which we find ourselves increasingly living lives that are not contained within national boundaries, increasingly able to be aware of the fate of populations geographically distant from ourselves, and increasingly able take action that will make a difference to the well-being of those populations, is a world in which the issue of global norms will be experienced ever more keenly. Clearly, then, the pressures on us to think globally, rather than merely locally or regionally, have increased, are increasing, and are unlikely to diminish.

If our world is one in which the development of global norms is likely to be a matter of increasing rather than decreasing concern, what does the future hold for global cultural diversity? The forces of globalisation that press the case for global norms are also sometimes conceived as forces that will erode the cultural diversities that make the development of global norms problematic. We might therefore suppose that, as there becomes ever more occasion for the development of global norms, so there will be a gradual disappearance of cultural diversities that might inhibit that development. But, even if that turns out to be the long-term fate of the world's cultural differences, it is a fate that still seems extremely distant. For the foreseeable future, the problem of how we should combine global norms with diverse cultures will remain a problem with which we shall have to wrestle; we cannot simply wait for the passage of time to dispose of the problem for us.

NOTES

1. We are grateful to the University of Newcastle for the award of a grant supporting the colloquium.

2

Cosmopolitanism, World Citizenship and Global Civil Society

CHRIS BROWN

We are told that Diogenes the Cynic was the first person to say 'I am a *kosmopolitês*', that is to say a 'citizen of the world (or universe)'; stoics, such as the Emperor Marcus Aurelius, preferred the full version, *politês tou kosmou*, but it is to Diogenes that we owe the term cosmopolitan (Nussbaum 1997: 53). His thought was the product of a period in which the old meaning of citizenship, being a *politês*, had been undermined. Previously, for a Greek of classical times, his (and it was 'his') partnership with his fellows in a *polis* was the most important feature of his identity. To live together in a city ruling oneself and being ruled in turn was at the heart of human flourishing, essential to happiness in a broad sense of that term; the human animal is a *zoon politikon* as Aristotle put it – this is usually translated as a 'political (or political and social) animal', but this loses some of the force of what is being said. Rather, the implication is that it is not possible to be human outside of the *polis*; the *polis* is prior in nature to each of us individually as well as to the households of which we are part. '[A] man who is incapable of entering into partnership, or who is so self-sufficing that he has no need to do so, is no part of a state, so that he must be either a lower animal or a god.' (Aristotle 1926–65: *Politics* I, 1. 12.) Furthermore, this partnership is not a commercial arrangement

This paper was first presented at a colloquium on Global Norms and Diverse Cultures at the University of Newcastle, 4–5 January 1999. A later version was presented in a seminar series on Postnational Democracy at the University of Bremen on 31 May 1999. I am grateful to both sets of participants, and to Dr Molly Cochran of the Georgia Institute of Technology, Atlanta, and to Peter Calvert, Andrew Mason and David Owen, all of the University of Southampton, for comments.

or a private association – it involves the capacity to determine the general arrangements of the city, the 'public thing' (res publica) as the Romans later put it.

Given these connotations, Diogenes' claim is, on the face of it, absurd. No more than there is now was there then a partnership of free individuals determining the general arrangements of the world – far from it, in place of the old Greek cities the Hellenic world was dominated by tyrannies and empires, and by the time of Marcus by one great empire, of which he was emperor. But, of course, Diogenes knew this, indeed, it was precisely because the cities had gone under that he was able to call himself a 'citizen of the world'. He is not setting up an opposition between being a kosmopolitês and being an Athenian, Theban or whatever, because there were no more 'Athenians' in the old sense of the term; instead, there were 'people who lived in Athens' under the rule of an external force, which was not the same thing at all. Diogenes is using a figure of speech, a metaphor; his attitude toward the world is like the attitude of the politês toward his fellows – he regards all of humanity as his fellow citizens. For a metaphor to work, the analogy on which it is based has to have some plausibility; in this case, the link is tenuous and the figure only made sense because the memory of genuine citizenship was fast fading. In any event, Nussbaum tells us, Diogenes had no interest in political thought, indeed, was wholly unpolitical, so was presumably not very interested in whether the metaphor made sense or not. By the time a Roman emperor can claim to be a citizen of the world, apparently with a straight face, we have to assume that the original meaning of citizenship had been completely lost.

The term 'cosmopolitan' was revived in the eighteenth century by the enlightened, especially by Kant, and is widely used today. Nussbaum herself employs it in the controversy she generated in the pages of the Boston Review with her essay 'Patriotism and Cosmopolitanism', the aim of which is to argue for an education which goes beyond the shared values expressed in an appeal to patriotism (Nussbaum 1996). As she is well aware, there is, of course, no world republic to replace the American Republic; indeed, she knows, as Diogenes knew, that 'the invitation to think as a world citizen was, in a sense, an invitation to be an exile from the comfort of patriotism and its easy sentiments' (Nussbaum 1996: 7). Nonetheless, by using the metaphor she opens herself up to a response that denies the analogy upon which the metaphor is based. Michael Walzer, in the same debate, does this very effectively by taking the figure literally:

> I am not a citizen of the world as she would like me to be. I am
> not even aware that there is a world such that one could be a
> citizen of it. No-one has ever offered me citizenship, or described
> the naturalisation process, or enlisted me in the world's
> institutional structures, or given me an account of its decision
> procedures (I hope they are democratic) or provided me with a
> list of the benefits and obligations of citizenship, or shown me the
> world's calendar and the common celebrations and
> commemorations of its citizens. (Walzer 1996: 125.)

He is, of course, deliberately pushing the point not because he thinks
that Nussbaum thinks these requirements could be met, but because he
(along with others) finds the metaphor unhelpful, misleading, even
dangerous. Nussbaum (along with others) disagrees and so the debate
is joined, here and elsewhere (Cohen 1996).

The purpose of these reflections is to act as a prelude to the
consideration of circumstances where another, quite similar, metaphor
is employed, but where it is by no means clear that the authors who use
it realise that they actually are employing a figure of speech.
Nowadays, the phrase 'global civil society' is, as it were, in the air.
Richard Falk writes of an existing transnational and an emergent global
civil society (Falk 1995: 170). David Held thinks this is 'a little
premature', but develops a project for cosmopolitan democracy which
would surely require such a foundation (Held 1995: 125). Michael
Walzer has edited a collection entitled *Toward a Global Civil Society*,
and Mervyn Frost has presented several conference papers with this
title; the present writer has also employed the term (Walzer 1995;
Frost 1998; Brown 1998). Theorists of globalisation have written of
global civil society, or some variant thereof, often in connection with
environmental problems (Lipschutz 1996; Wapner 1996). Some
critical security theorists look to an embryonic global civil society
(Booth 1991). One way or another, the notion of global civil society
seems to many people to be the answer to at least some of the world's
ills, whatever the latter might be.

What do these writers mean by the (emergent, embryonic) global
(transnational) civil society? Some crisp definitions appear in the
literature, for example, '*Transnational civil society* in this context
refers to a set of interactions among an imagined community to shape
collective life that are not confined to the territorial and institutional

spaces of states.' (Price 1998: 615.) But a more elaborate, less sophisticated account may be of greater use here. The background assumption to all of this work is that there now exists a globalised (or, at least, internationalised) economy upon which global civil society rests. Thereafter, four factors seem to appear in most accounts: the existence of an extensive network of intergovernmental organisations, allegedly providing a framework for global governance; the existence of informal, non-state, transnational pressure groups, most frequently in the area of the environment, but also encompassing human rights, animal rights and so on; cross-cultural global trends in consumption, entertainment and 'infotainment'; and, lastly, some kind of normative foundation for these factors, possibly epitomised by the human rights regime. On this account, it should be noted, global civil society is different from, on the one hand, 'international society', the norm-governed relations of states, and, on the other, the global spread of civil society domestically, although it is obviously related to both, especially the second, of these two phenomena.

Now, we might argue about the significance, or even the existence, of some of the factors listed above, but a more fundamental point is whether, taken together, they amount to even an emergent global 'civil society'. We have seen how the idea of world citizenship emerges from, but leaves some way behind, the original meaning of citizenship. Civil society also has or had an original meaning – is the same process happening here? The purpose of this essay is to investigate this question. The origins and original meaning of the term 'civil society' will be explored with a view to establishing the basis upon which the analogy reflected in the metaphor of a global civil society is constructed. Then, the appropriateness of this analogy will be examined. To anticipate the argument somewhat, the position provisionally adopted below is that while it is just possible that it might make sense to think of an emergent North Atlantic civil society, the extension of the metaphor to *global* civil society is profoundly misleading. Moreover, it is misleading not simply on the kind of quantitative grounds that lead some writers to be cautious about the use of the term (the web of global governance and private transactions not yet being thick enough to sustain the metaphor), but, more fundamentally, it is misleading because civil society is, at one and the same time, both a social value and a set of institutions, and in the absence of the former, the latter cannot be expected to work (Hall 1995: 2). Moreover, the metaphor of global civil society draws attention away from areas where political action to create a more just world order might be more effective.

The Specificity of Civil Society

The notion of 'civil society' is prefigured in the works of Hobbes and Locke, but is, at root, a product of eighteenth-century thought, most obviously that of the later Scottish Enlightenment (where the key statement is Adam Ferguson's *An Essay on the History of Civil Society*), although the notion also appears in the writings of the Marquis de Montesquieu, and is given its most elaborate (and contentious) expression in the thought of G.W.F. Hegel, especially in the *Philosophy of Right* (Ferguson 1966; Hegel 1991). The most minimal and negative definition of civil society involves the idea of society organising itself separately from and set against the state. This idea has, of course, been present throughout the history of the past 200 years, but it took on particular significance in the 1980s at the point at which it became clear that the Marxist project of fusing state and society was not simply inimical to any plausible idea of freedom, but also incapable of sustaining a modern economy – the inability of the Soviet Union either to feed itself or to compete in technological terms with the west lay behind its collapse, even though the process of collapse itself owed as much to contingencies as to this long-term weakness. In the post-Marxist, east-central European world of the end of the 1980s, 'civil society' was seen to be the key that would open the door to a free and prosperous future, a belief which was fed by an extensive new literature on the subject (Keane 1988). Not surprisingly, given the claims made on behalf of the notion, something of a reaction set in, with some sociologists in the west arguing that the term had been prised away from its original meaning in ways that hampered, rather than aided, comprehension (Kumar 1993). However, by the mid-1990s a somewhat more balanced picture had emerged, marked by the publication of an authoritative collection of essays edited by John Hall, which was specifically designed to try to counteract both the overenthusiasm of adherents in the 1980s and the dismissal of the notion by their critics (Hall 1995). The account of civil society presented here draws heavily on this collection, and on the very forceful, but slightly more idiosyncratic, work of Ernest Gellner (1994).

The very crude, negative definition of civil society presented above is unsatisfactory in two main respects. First, it misses the complexity of the relationship between civil society and the state; this point is well made in a more extended definition of civil society offered by Gellner (although not one that he regards as satisfactory, for reasons which will be discussed below):

> [Civil] society is that set of non-governmental institutions, which is strong enough to counterbalance the state, and, whilst not preventing the state from fulfilling the role of keeper of the peace and arbitrator between major interests, can, nevertheless, prevent the state from dominating and atomising the rest of society. (Gellner 1994: 5.)

The point is that although civil society sets bounds upon, and limits the activities of, the state, it nonetheless requires that there be an effective state for it to limit and set bounds upon. In the absence of peace, and without some mechanism outside of itself for arbitration between major interests, civil society cannot exist – a point highly relevant to the Mafia-ridden reality of the post-Soviet Russian Republic. Civil society stands against despotism and tyranny, but actually requires a strong(ish) state, albeit a state governed by the rule of law.

Why is the above, extended definition unsatisfactory? Gellner suggests that it tells only half the story, implying that tyranny is necessarily tied to strong central institutions; not so, there are many examples of plural societies, with weak or non-existent central authorities, based on kinship, in which 'tyranny by cousins' replaces tyranny by kings. Civil society is radically distinct from 'the segmentary community which avoids central tyranny by firmly turning the individual into an integral part of the social sub-unit' (Gellner 1994: 8). Thus, civil society stands against decentralised kinship-based agrarian societies as firmly as it stands against over-centralised tyrannies; but it also stands against ancient republican societies which were 'free' (assuming you were an adult male and not a slave), but which possessed, as it were, the wrong kind of freedom. Hall stresses this point – the idea that there can be some kind of alliance between modern proponents of civil society and the more extreme adherents of republican civic virtue is quite wrong; in principle, the two ideals are opposed to one another (Hall 1995: 10). The notion of civic virtue implies a degree of moral unity, a positive role for law and, *in extremis*, can lead to Rousseau's notion of forcing people to be free – a notion which, as translated by Marx and Lenin, lay behind the regimes that collapsed in the east in 1989–91. For the proponents of civil society, on the other hand, freedom involves a minimalist approach to law and the abandonment of the idea of managed consensus, whether managed by an authoritarian state, by stifling kinship bonds, or (less relevant in the context of this essay) by the standard-bearers of republican virtue.

Thus, for civil society to function, what is required is a state which is 'strong', in the sense that it is capable of preserving order and enforcing the law, but not too 'strong', in the sense of being so extensive in its reach that it is capable of posing a continuing serious threat to civil liberties and the autonomy of non-state institutions. Such a state must be populated by individuals who are determined to live private lives and pursue private goals, tolerant of each other, and willing to join private associations, but resistant to being corralled into 'social cages' (Hall 1995: 15). There is very little margin for error here – if the state is too extensive it will strangle civil society at birth, too weak and private institutions will compete for its role as provider of order; if people are too much involved in each other's lives then they lose the sense of distance needed to preserve civility, too little involved and they become part of an atomised 'mass society'.

It is hardly surprising that the conditions for the emergence of civil society have, on this account, occurred only once, in some parts of western Europe toward the latter half of the eighteenth century. Because of the peculiar history of power relations in Europe (the incomplete collapse of the Roman Empire, the multiple power structures of the middle ages, the incomplete achievement of absolutist power after the ending of the middle ages, and the need for European states to garner popular support to underpin their external policies) some European states at this time met the 'effective, but not too extensive' criterion sketched above. Because of the growth of mercantile capitalism, a wealth-seeking bourgeoisie combined with an aristocracy increasingly oriented toward a commercial approach to landowning to create a culture in which private enrichment was considered normal. Because of the costs of the wars of religion and the inability of (especially Protestant) rulers to enforce conformity, an attitude of toleration came to be widespread. Civil society emerged. It should be noted that this account is much more modest in its claims for this society than is Habermas's not altogether dissimilar account of the emergence of the 'public sphere' in the same time-frame (Habermas 1989). Habermas is inclined to see this process in terms of democratisation, which is reading too much into the achievement of civil society, and to see the 'public sphere' as restraining the state, whereas on the account presented above, civil society emerges because, for one reason or another, the state is already (somewhat) restrained.

The fact that civil society emerged then and there tells us little about its subsequent fate. It may be that civil society could only have emerged in these circumstances, but once having emerged, it might be possible for it to be transplanted elsewhere. Nor, to continue the metaphor, is it necessary that soil conditions elsewhere duplicate those of its place of origin; civil society may be able to assist in creating the conditions under which a transplant is possible. But, nonetheless, it is a fragile plant, and the general climate is not usually favourable to it establishing itself. Both Gellner and Habermas, in their different ways, see the rise of industrial society as threatening some aspects of civil society by placing too much power in the hands of giant, unaccountable institutions. Gellner adds other limiting or problematic features of particular significance to the argument in this essay.

First, he stresses the importance of the general state of the international system. One of the reasons why civil society was able to establish itself in the first place was because states were engaged in interstate rivalry and required at least some support from the wealthier segment of their populations, which gave the latter a certain bargaining power. More to the point, one of the reasons that civil society has been able to survive has been the existence of numerous separate jurisdictions, such that if civil society were threatened in one it could survive in others (the loss of civil society in Germany in 1933 and its re-establishment post-1948 is the paradigm case for this process). Gellner regards the spread of globalisation as undermining this latter possibility – from now on, if civil society is lost anywhere it is likely to be lost everywhere. This argument almost certainly overstates the (current) importance of globalisation, but, nonetheless, is a useful restatement of the value of the existence of multiples centres of power in the international system.

Second, more worrying for most modern liberals, Gellner stresses the shallow roots of the liberal values on which civil society is based, in particular, the notion of tolerance and the importance of personal autonomy. Most people are not keen to live under the tyranny of kings, or their modern equivalents, but the attractions of belonging are very strong and the desire to be part of a community goes very deep. In the eighteenth century, enlightened intellectuals wanted to keep their distance from the wider society, but whether this was ever a popular end can be doubted, and from the nineteenth century onward, 'alienation' has become something to be avoided rather than sought. Most societies have valued order above either economic growth or political liberty and so have most people. It is an illusion to think that the truth that he himself finds in liberal thought has, Gellner argues, in itself any power, and the Enlightenment belief that a social order without coercion and falsehood is possible is equally illusory. Any culture is a systematic prejudgement; the miracle of civil society is that, for once, and in exceptional circumstances, the prejudgement was made milder and flexible, and yet order was maintained (Gellner 1994: 32). This is an achievement that is continually under threat, especially since the continued growth of the wealth with which civil society has supported itself (bought off some of its opponents and defeated others) is, potentially, put in question by the emergence of environmental limits to growth.

As suggested above, Gellner's position is a little idiosyncratic, but it forms a useful corrective to the more gung-ho, decontextualised, oversimplified account peddled by the snake-oil salespersons of post-Marxism, for whom civil society was the remedy for all ills, the relatively painless route from totalitarianism to the sunlit uplands of contemporary post-industrial society. His account rests much more on Ferguson than it does on Hegel, but it is worth noting that Hegel, like Gellner, sees a strong, constitutional state as a necessary counterpart to civil society, and stresses the importance of an interstate system (Hegel 1991). The important points to take away from the work of Gellner, Hall and others is that civil society is a fragile social formation, that not every set of structures that stands against the state can be seen as promoting civil society, and that there are important values which are a precondition for its survival. The next section of this essay will examine the implications of these points for the notion of global civil society.

Global Civil Society and Global Governance

Promoters of the notion of an emerging global civil society generally see the growth of global governance as part of the process, by which they mean the growth of international institutions attempting to regulate and coordinate global social and economic interactions. The argument here is essentially 'functionalist' (Mitrany 1975). The emerging web of rules and regulations created by these institutions is taken to provide the backdrop against which the real business of global civil society (the activities of autonomous non-state institutions) can take place. There is a reluctance on the part of writers on globalisation generally to see this network as a real government, much less a state; the term 'governance' is generally used instead of 'government' in this context. That there is no global government in the full sense of that term is clearly the case, and is taken for granted by the promoters of global civil society, who generally do not see this absence as problematic. In this they are mistaken.

In the first place, to state the obvious, it is clear that there are major 'law and order' problems in the international system, and these problems severely restrict the functioning of global civil society. Apart from the obvious inability of global civil society to function in more than a very limited way during actual wars, even in 'peacetime' autonomous non-state institutions need more than a network of international civil and commercial law in order to function. They also need the protection of a police force and at the moment the only such bodies are provided by the individual states, and in many parts of the world are, at best, extremely ineffective, at worst, wholly corrupt. There are two trends that have emerged from this, both, in different ways, damaging to the idea of civil society. First, in recent years, increasing numbers of individuals employed by non-state bodies (employees of business corporations, human rights activists, and aid workers) have been attacked, kidnapped or killed while going about their work in sub-Saharan Africa or Latin America. Second, in response to this kind of danger, many of the richer non-state organisations (especially, of course, private economic actors) have taken to providing their own 'security' by striking unsavoury deals with local Mafias (official or unofficial), by setting up dedicated private police forces, or by employing one or other of the private military companies that have sprung up in recent years. In each case, forces that are difficult to control are unleashed or strengthened; these forces 'tax' in order to provide selective protection, as opposed to the general protection that an effective system of law and order ought to provide. Initially a response to the lack of effective local law and order, the privatisation of security soon itself becomes an obstacle to the establishment of the latter, by providing the means for some of the most important actors to, in effect, drop out of the local political system. All this is clearly inimical to the chances of establishing a global civil society.

Second, and equally damaging to the prospects of civil society, is the absence of an international arbitrator between powerful private global interests. One of the obvious points about the operation of a civil society is that the non-state institutions of which it is largely composed have different, and frequently conflicting, interests. A major role of the state is to arbitrate these interests, either actively by intervening in the contest directly or passively by providing the framework in which the contest takes place, including a background of relevant information which might affect the course of the conflict. In the absence of any international body capable of performing this function, outcomes of conflicts between non-state institutions will be shaped by the success or failure of these bodies in deploying the resources they possess, including their ability to capture public opinion in significant states. Usually, this means that non-state economic actors will dominate, but not always – it is worth noting, for example, that Greenpeace International is often capable of capturing public opinion and using it against, for example, the giant oil companies, even in circumstances where the latter are operating in good faith and on the basis of the best scientific opinion. Similarly, bodies such as international aid agencies, private and public, can, in conjunction with newscasters such as CNN, capture and direct international attention toward the issues that most concern them at the time, which are not always those which an independent arbitrator would choose to prioritise. At the time of writing (July 1999), the media are, perhaps understandably, much exercised by the aftermath of the war in Kosovo, but conditions in parts of sub-Saharan Africa (especially, at the moment, Angola) are much worse. Similarly, the destruction caused by hurricanes Georges and Mitch in the Caribbean in the autumn of 1998, horrendous though it was, received disproportionate attention compared to the equally catastrophic floods in Bangladesh at the same time. Private infotainment corporations provide the news they believe their audience will want to see, and in so doing shape the global agenda in ways that an arbiter might wish to contest.

Both in the case of the privatisation of security and in the case of the consequences of the absence of any body capable of articulating a 'global public interest' to check the private interests of non-state institutional actors, what we see is that the agents of a putative global civil society are obliged to turn themselves into substitutes for a global state. In so doing they overstep themselves, becoming part of the problem rather than part of the solution. Rather than providing a space in which private citizens can live private lives and, simultaneously, limit the scope of state activity, these institutions become a substitute for the global state, but an ineffective and anti-democratic substitute, and one, moreover, always likely to be overridden on key issues by the ultimate power-holders in the system, the major states.

The one part of the world where it is possible to trace the emergence of what looks like a civil society is the North Atlantic region: the USA and Canada along with the European Union and fellow travellers of the latter such as Norway and Switzerland. Here, each of the countries concerned is a constitutional state governed by quite similar legal codes and with police forces and judiciaries that are reasonably effective and impartial – citizens of these states and non-state institutions can expect their positions to be protected everywhere throughout the North Atlantic region. Moreover, a half-century of co-operation on economic matters in bodies such as the EU, but also in the OECD, GATT/WTO, the IMF and the World Bank, have lessened the differences between and among these societies, while the co-operation of most of them in NATO has produced a common solution to problems of security within the area. It may be that there is no 'state' to complement a North Atlantic civil society, but the high level of co-operation in the region provides a more-or-less effective substitute for such a state authority – law and order is maintained and interests are arbitrated. However, *pace* Shaw, the evidence of the post-cold-war years does not suggest that this *ad hoc* set of arrangements is capable of being converted into an *international* state capable of performing law-and-order and arbitrator functions on a global stage (Shaw 1994).

Global Norms, Diverse Cultures and Global Civil Society

The North Atlantic region is that part of the world with the most developed infrastructure of non-state international institutions and the highest level of security – it is a zone of peace and stability in a much less secure and less stable world, and as such it has some of the preconditions for the emergence of a regional civil society. But, as well as these institutional features, the North Atlantic region is, of course, also the cultural home of the idea of civil society; here, if anywhere, one might expect that the set of attitudes necessary for a civil society to function would be found, and this is, indeed, more or less the case. It would be a mistake to exaggerate the extent to which the values associated with civil society still permeate North Atlantic societies, but, at the very least, significant traces remain. The development of industrial society and the growth of the mass media have made it more difficult for either the 'public sphere' envisaged by Habermas or the private sphere envisaged by Gellner to survive, but the social 'prejudgement' in favour of a degree of tolerance identified by the latter is still just about present. Partly because this is so, the notion of civil society is not misapplied in this regional context.

For the most part, outside of this region, these cultural preconditions do not exist, or at least exist only in a very weak form. Few doubt the truth of this generalisation – one of the reasons why most cautious writers talk of an 'emerging' or 'nascent' global civil society is because they recognise that the values needed to sustain such an entity are not yet sufficiently widespread, or deeply held, to allow one to make the claim that it exists already. Rather, the hope and expectation of such writers is that these values are in the process of being created, and, indeed, one of the roles of the emergent civil society is precisely to assist in creating the conditions needed for its own reproduction. This is a two-pronged process, although it should be said that the two 'prongs' rarely recognise that they are part of the same process. On the one hand, the combined efforts of international business to make profits and of international economic organisations to regulate the world economy have the side-effect of promoting a conception of private property rights and of the limits of state action which might be thought of as providing part of the background to the development of a global civil society; on the other hand, rather more obviously, the international human rights regime is promoted by non-state groups to the same ultimate end. It is possible to doubt whether either prong is quite as successful as its adherents might wish (global economic processes seem as likely to provoke resistance as compliance with the new economic norms, as Benjamin Barber has noted, and the extent to which the human rights regime is capable of penetrating cultural barriers can be doubted), but, nonetheless, genuine movement has taken place, to the extent that Mervyn Frost can write, not altogether implausibly, of a drive toward development and an acceptance of universal human rights as 'settled norms' of contemporary international society (Barber 1996; Brown 1997a; Frost 1996).

But even if one accepts the force of this argument, is it actually the case that the spread of liberal attitudes to property and human rights is a sufficient condition for the establishment of a successful civil society? Up to a point, certainly, but it would not be difficult to imagine the emergence of societies where this spread had taken place and where civil society had, apparently, been established, but where so many of the intangibles involved in the notion were missing that social relations never really worked out the way they were supposed to, where tolerance was required by law but not internalised by the people, where the capacity to live a private life was guaranteed in principle but difficult to operationalise in practice, and where the freedoms that did exist were always at the mercy of a downturn in economic conditions. Indeed, putting aside the spread of civil society beyond Europe and its former colonies, some Habermasian lines of argument suggest that this is more or less where North Atlantic societies are today (Habermas 1989; Arato and Cohen 1992).

The societies of the North Atlantic region do, at least, have a tradition of viewing themselves in the ambiguous, ironic, nuanced way that is essential for the preservation of toleration. This 'civilised' frame of mind and 'civility' in the sense of manners is very important here, and still survives even if the peculiar mix of forces which created civil society in the eighteenth century (Protestantism and non-conformity combined with the progress of commerce and manufactures) have much less resonance today than then. The point is that civil society requires a particular kind of human being in order to function successfully: an individual who is capable of making *ad hoc*, but effective, commitments to limited associations for particular purposes without these associations coming to dominate his or her life, someone who can hold opinions firmly and act upon them but is prepared to change them in response to changing circumstances – 'it is *this* which makes Civil Society: the forging of links which are effective even though they are flexible, specific, instrumental' (Gellner 1994: 100).

Such a cast of mind is comparatively unusual, as has been the political freedom with which it is associated. More usually, humans find themselves in complex social relationships where associations are meant to be taken deadly seriously and where 'opinion' cannot be changed without danger, where flexible, instrumental links are regarded as no links at all. Alternatively, once these deeper associations break down, individuals emerge into a state of atomisation in mass society. In neither case can the kind of freedom associated with civil society be established with any serious chance of long-run success, even if some of the institutions associate with civil society (the private business corporation and individual human rights) can be established. Civil society is a mind-set as well as a set of institutions; in the long-to-medium run, it is not possible to have the latter without the former.

Many non-European societies today do not want to develop this mind-set, even though they may want some of the benefits that go with it. Undoubtedly, a great deal of the discourse of 'Asian' or 'African' values is designed to protect the interests of local power brokers, but at the heart of this discourse is a desire to preserve a way of life in which people do not regard their associations as limited and flexible, a desire to preserve community in a deeper sense than is available via civil society. Nor ought this to be thought of as necessarily an ignoble desire. As Duncan Forbes remarks of Adam Smith and Adam Ferguson, they saw the:

> paradox of the progress of commerce and manufactures giving rise on the one hand to personal liberty and security, the blessings of the rule of law, but at the same time and equally inevitably producing a second-rate sort of society full of second-rate citizens pursuing comparatively worthless objects (Forbes 1966: xiii).

This is a deeply serious point which deserves to be reiterated; if people have personal liberty and security guaranteed by law, and thus have the capacity to define their own project in life, there is no reason to think that they will use this freedom to pursue edifying ends, or that the society they produce will be particularly attractive. The point about free people is that they are free, not that they are good, or sensible, or pleasant to know. Even people who have experienced the freedom of civil society may well be persuaded to give it up if they become convinced that personal liberty is worth trading in for a sense of belonging in a wider community (Germany in 1933) and those who already possess the latter may value it more highly than the former. An ironic, unheroic disposition is less prevalent than those who give their allegiance to western civil societies might expect or hope.

Civil Society and Political Action

To summarise the argument thus far, civil society is the fragile achievement of a small number of western societies, under some threat 'at home' and unlikely to spread further afield without a very radical change in the ways in which most human beings form themselves and desire to live. For this reason, and because of the absence of an international political counterpart to the domestic state, to apply the notion of civil society to developments globally is a mistake, a metaphor that misleads rather than illuminates. The only place where anything resembling 'global' civil society is to be found is in the interrelations of those countries where civil society is already established at a local level. Nor is this state of affairs likely to change in the near future – the gap between the existing state of affairs and a global civil society is not quantitative but qualitative. It is not the case that a global civil society is 'emerging' from the *status quo* as part of the processes of globalisation. Possibly some wider global, social, co-operative arrangements will emerge, but there is no reason to think they will have the characteristics normally associated with civil society.

Assuming, perhaps implausibly, that this argument is accepted, does it matter? Perhaps the notion of a global civil society is based on an inappropriate analogy between international and domestic political life, but those who have developed the notion are unlikely to be devastated by this criticism. They believe that the interactions they are promoting are desirable in their own right (and in this they may be correct, at least some of the time) and whether these relationships are to be thought of as constituting a civil society they would take to be an academic question in the pejorative sense of that term. Perhaps this is a case of taking too seriously what is little more than a figure of speech? One objection to this line of argument is that it is intellectually unhealthy to use words in such a way that they lose contact with their original meaning, but a more compelling response is that the misuse of the term 'civil society', the misunderstanding of what is involved in establishing civil society, is responsible for some quite serious mistakes in the realm of political action.

The notion of global civil society has become quite popular in some circles, at least in part, because other routes toward a more equitable and just world order seem to be closed off. In international relations theory, the project of international institutional reform which was so central in the early years of the discipline has now been marginalised. The notion that one can achieve 'world peace through world law' has been a casualty of the victory of 'realist' theories of international relations (Clark and Sohn 1966; Brown 1997b: 21–39). At the same time, it often seems that in many, perhaps most, parts of the world (*in extremis*, perhaps everywhere) as far as equity and justice is concerned, the state is the problem rather than part of the solution, the agent of exploitation and oppression rather than the guarantor of welfare and civil liberties. Given these two parameters, it is not surprising that people of good will have looked to the emergence of global civil society to place a check on the state, and to try to act as a substitute for global political arrangements that cannot be achieved by any direct route; much the same line of reasoning lay behind the western promotion of the notion of civil society in post-Communist eastern Europe. The burden of this essay is that this is not a sensible strategy. Global civil society will only emerge when and if domestic civil societies emerge on a global scale and there are quite good reasons to think that this is unlikely to take place within any plausible time-scale, if at all. Putting too much investment into the notion of global civil society is likely to lead to frustration at best, or at worst to the legitimisation of the exercise of power by unaccountable, undemocratic non-state actors (or of governments which take excessive power in the name of combating such external forces). The paradigm cases here are, on the one hand, those parts of sub-Saharan Africa where international business corporations have taken over the security functions of the state and exercise them in their own sectional interests and, on the other, those Asian authoritarian capitalist states where the uncontrolled power of local rulers is justified by them in terms of the necessity to preserve society from the depredations of international speculators and western cultural imperialists.

A re-emphasis on state-building (which was, after all, a major focus of the immediate post-colonial era) would make a great deal more sense than efforts to buttress the allegedly emerging institutions of global civil society; indeed, such an emphasis would be quite compatible with the long-term goal of creating the circumstances under which such a society might emerge. In the first context mentioned above, it is clear that the only effective way to combat the spreading privatisation of security in regions such as West Africa is for western nations to put as much effort as possible into assisting local states to develop effective security forces of their own – even, possibly, in some circumstances where state governments are non-democratic. The basic (Hobbesian) position that any effective government is better than no government may not be entirely acceptable (ask the survivors of the Rwanda state-sponsored genocide), but is close to the truth (ask the peoples of Liberia, or Somalia, or any other society riven by civil war). In countries where effective, but authoritarian, state structures exist, there is a case for directing assistance toward those forces which are attempting to make these systems more accountable, but it is important that effectiveness is not lost in this process. The riots and killing of ethnic Chinese in Indonesia in the spring of 1998 give a taste of what can very easily happen if the process of democratisation causes the state to lose control. The central point in both these different sets of circumstances is that, in terms of the basic security of the individual, the protection afforded by effective state structures is a precondition for every other development, and too much emphasis on building civil society is either irrelevant or positively harmful if it directs resources away from the primary task of establishing such structures.

As well as a re-emphasis on state-building, a return to the older project of *international institutional reform* may also be desirable. It is certainly implausible to think in terms of developing the UN into a genuine world government, but there is scope for a degree of institutional reform at this level. Even within the existing Charter, it would not take more than a minor shift of emphasis to bring about real change – as the case of the Rwanda demonstrates, where a slightly less risk-averse UN might well have prevented the genocide altogether (Jones 1995; *New York Times* 1998). The establishment of a semi-permanent UN peace-keeping force would be one such move; the creation of a Genocide Commission specifically tasked to prevent the Security Council from averting its eyes in circumstances such as those in Rwanda would be another. Such reforms, although oriented toward an interstate body and in no sense looking to transcend the present international order, would not necessarily be incompatible with the growing interest in finding an *institutional* base for cosmopolitan democracy manifested in the work of David Held or Andrew Linklater (Held 1995; Linklater 1998). The key point is that an interest in parallel cosmopolitan political forms and in *post*-Westphalian citizenship ought not to be allowed to draw attention away from the pressing need to create a less violent interstate order in which the benefits of *Westphalian* citizenship are available to a larger number of people than is, at present, the case.

As this last point suggests, the argument here is ultimately not that the idea of global civil society is unimportant or irrelevant, rather that it ought not to be allowed to substitute for a less indirect approach to the political problems of our contemporary international order. The problems of violence and injustice in that order are not such that they can be put on one side while a new and better world is designed. The response that these problems require is a renewed emphasis on the political forms which need to be in place and functioning effectively, domestically and internationally, before the question of a global civil society can even be put, let alone answered in the affirmative.

REFERENCES

Arato, A. and Cohen, J. 1992, *Civil Society and Democratic Theory*. Cambridge (MA): MIT Press.

Aristotle. 1926–65, *Politics*. London: Loeb Classical Library, Heinemann.

Barber, B. 1996, *Jihad vs. McWorld: How Globalisation and Tribalism are Reshaping the World*. New York: Ballantine.

Booth, K. 1991. Security and emancipation. *Review of International Studies*, Vol.17, No.4, pp.313–26.

Brown, C. 1997a. Universal human rights: a critique. *International Journal of Human Rights*, Vol.1, No.2, pp.41–65.

1997b, *Understanding International Relations*. London: Macmillan.

1998. Justice and international order. Paper presented to the UK Association for Legal and Social Philosophy, Twenty-Fifth Annual Conference.

Clark, G. and Sohn, S.B. 1966, *World Peace through World Law*. Cambridge (MA): Harvard University Press.

Cohen, J. ed. 1996, *For Love of Country: Debating the Limits of Patriotism*. Boston: Beacon Press.

Falk, R., 1995. The world order between inter-state law and the law of humanity: the role of civil society institutions. In *Cosmopolitan Democracy: An Agenda for a New World Order*, ed. Archibugi, D. and Held, D. Cambridge, Polity Press.

Ferguson, A. 1966, *An Essay on the History of Civil Society*. Edinburgh: Edinburgh University Press.

Forbes, D., 1966. Introduction to Ferguson. In *An Essay on the History of Civil Society*. Edinburgh, Edinburgh University Press.

Frost, M. 1996, *Ethics in International Relations*. Cambridge: Cambridge University Press.

1998. Global civil society. Joint ISA/ECPR Standing Group on IR Conference, Vienna.

Gellner, E. 1994, *Conditions of Liberty: Civil Society and its Rivals*. London: Hamish Hamilton.

1995. The importance of being modular. In *Civil Society*, ed. Hall, J.A. Cambridge, Polity Press.

Habermas, J. 1989, *The Structural Transformation of the Public Sphere*. Cambridge (MA): MIT Press.

Hall, J.A. ed. 1995, *Civil Society*. Cambridge: Polity Press.

Hegel, G.W.F. 1991, *Elements of the Philosophy of Right*. Cambridge: Cambridge University Press.

Held, D. 1995, *Democracy and the Global Order*. Cambridge: Polity Press.

Jones, B.A. 1995. 'Intervention without borders': humanitarian intervention in Rwanda, 1990–94. *Millennium: Journal of International Studies*, Vol.24, No.2, pp.225–51.

Keane, J. ed. 1988, *Civil Society and the State: New European Perspectives*. London: Verso.

Kumar, K. 1993. Civil society: an enquiry into the usefulness of a historical term. *British Journal of Sociology*, Vol.44, No.3, pp.375–95.

Linklater, A. 1998, *The Transformation of Political Community*. Cambridge: Polity Press.

Lipschutz, R.D. 1996, *Global Civil Society and Global Environmental Governance*. Albany (NY): State University of New York Press.

Mitrany, D. 1975, *The Functional Theory of Politics*. London: Martin Robertson.

New York Times. 1998. General tells Rwanda court massacre was preventable, 28 February 1998.

Nussbaum, M., 1996. Patriotism and cosmopolitanism. In *For Love of Country: Debating the Limits of Patriotism*, ed. Cohen, J. Boston, Beacon Press.

1997. Kant and cosmopolitanism. In *Perpetual Peace: Essays on Kant's Cosmopolitan Ideal*, ed. Bohman, J. and Lutz-Bachman, M. Cambridge (MA), MIT Press.

Price, R. 1998. Reversing the gun sights: transnational civil society targets land mines. *International Organisation*, Vol.52, No.4, pp.613–44.

Roberts, A. and Kingsbury, B. eds. 1993, *United Nations, Divided World*. Oxford: Clarendon Press.

Shaw, M. 1994, *Global Society and International Politics*. Cambridge: Polity Press.

Walzer, M. ed. 1995, *Toward a Global Civil Society*. Providence (RI): Berghahn.
  1996. Spheres of affection. In *For Love of Country: Debating the Limits of Patriotism*, ed. Cohen, J. Boston, Beacon Press.

Wapner, P. 1996, *Environmental Activism and World Civic Politics*. Albany (NY): State University of New York Press.

3

Human Rights and Diverse Cultures: Continuity or Discontinuity?

PETER JONES

The doctrine of human rights is necessarily a universalist doctrine. It ascribes a single set of rights to all humanity. Yet it has to assert its universal rights in a world characterised by diversity – a world in which people live in different circumstances, bear different cultures, and pursue different forms of life. At best, that diversity can seem inconvenient for, and at worst fatal to, the universality claimed for human rights.

In fact, a very large portion of human diversity is quite unproblematic for a theory of human rights. Human individuals exhibit different physical and personal characteristics, but that sort of diversity does not prevent our identifying all of those human beings as human and insisting that all are entitled to the same minimum of concern and respect merely as human beings. In addition, human beings exhibit differences as members of different societies and cultures, but, again, much of that diversity need not trouble the human rights theorist. Differences in diet, dress, leisure pursuits, literature, musical forms, and the like, do not prevent our claiming that the human beings that exhibit those differences possess a uniform set of rights as human beings. On the contrary, the rights commonly claimed for human beings would include rights to express and to pursue those differences. The supposition that a uniform set of rights must

This article was written during my tenure of a Nuffield Foundation Social Science Research Fellowship; I am grateful to the Foundation for its support. Earlier versions of the article were presented to a conference, Human Rights: Sacred or Secular?, held in 1998 at the Milltown Institute of Theology and Philosophy, Dublin, and to a Human Rights seminar at the University of Essex, as well as to the Newcastle colloquium on Global Norms and Diverse Cultures. I am indebted to the participants in those events for much helpful comment.

presuppose, or must make for, a uniform mode of life is quite mistaken.

So it is not human diversity in general that is troublesome for a theory of human rights. The troubles are caused by a particular type of diversity: diversity of belief and value. We live in a world in which people subscribe to different religious faiths and to different sects within each faith. We also find human beings embedded in cultures which differ in their understandings of the world and in what they prescribe for human life. But differences of belief and value do not stem only from differences in religion and culture. Even those who are supposed to belong to the same culture, or who subscribe to the same religious faith or to no religious faith, can disagree radically about how we should conduct our lives both individually and in relation to one another. The theorist of human rights has, then, to assert his universal values in a world in which values are subject to widespread disagreement.

How should the fact of diversity of belief and value affect our thinking about human rights? One reply might be, not at all. If we have good grounds for ascribing certain rights to human beings indifferently, there is no reason why we should forfeit or modify our commitment to those rights merely because others do not share it. Slavery, for example, is an institution that many in the past have endorsed and that some people still find acceptable; but the mere fact that others take no exception to slavery is no reason why we should forsake or compromise our belief that slavery is wrong. Catholics do not give up on Catholicism just because not everyone is a Catholic; Muslims do not forsake Islam merely because not everyone shares their faith. Why should the human rights theorist be any different?

Moreover, the doctrine of human rights is meant to be a fighting doctrine. Its purpose is not to leave the world as we find it, but to transform it into a better, more just world. A doctrine of human rights should challenge other ways of thinking; it should confront and seek to displace cultures and ideologies that fail to recognise human rights. We might conclude therefore that, while diversity of belief and value may prove troublesome when we try to implement a theory of human rights, it is utterly without consequence for the theory itself. It need make absolutely no difference to the foundation or form or content of a theory of human rights.

A second possible response is of a directly opposite kind. It holds that, rather than making no difference, the fact of diversity makes all the difference to a putative theory of human rights.[1] For many people, diversity of belief and value provides reason for rejecting any morality that aspires to universality, particularly a morality as ambitiously universal as the doctrine of human rights. Why should we give any more credence to the idea of human rights than to the many other moral notions presented to us by humanity? Why, if the case for human rights is as clear as its proponents would have us believe, has so much of humanity for so much of the time not recognised that case?

Even if it does not lead us to reject the doctrine of human rights out of hand, the fact of diversity may persuade us that it is an unduly arrogant and insensitive doctrine. Those who believe in human rights may have some justification for thinking as they do, but so too do the many adherents of the many other doctrines to be found across the globe. Yet, the human rights theorist typically claims a privileged status for his position. He is not content to place his theory alongside others and leave it to compete for our allegiance on equal terms with other theories. He insists that human rights must have an overriding status and that the prescriptions of other moralities should be ruled permissible in so far as they conform with, and impermissible in so far as they conflict with, the claims of human rights. Not only does he claim a unique status for his doctrine, the human rights theorist also insists that the institutions of the international community should be mobilised to spread and impose his doctrine across the world.

Yet, in spite of the human rights theorist's confidence in his own beliefs, there is often a suspicion that his doctrine is really just one doctrine among many, with no real claim to specialness. Indeed, the suspicion is often more specific: that the theory of human rights is a doctrine specific to the west during the modern era. It pretends to be a doctrine unique in status and universal in reach, but, in reality, it is no more than a local prejudice. Hence the familiar charge of cultural imperialism. The theory of human rights pretends to speak for all, but it is really no more than a doctrine of some, and a doctrine that is all the more insidious for the way in which it licenses its own imposition upon the whole of humanity.

Accommodating Disagreement

Are these two diametrically opposed ways of reading the juxtaposition of human rights and human diversity the only ones available to us? Can a theory of human rights recognise and accommodate the fact of human diversity, yet retain substance and credibility as a theory of human rights? Before trying to answer that question, we need to address another: should a theory of human rights respond to the fact of human diversity? Clearly, there would be no point in developing a theory designed to accommodate diverse beliefs and values if that accommodation were something we should not attempt. So why should a theory of human rights take account of people's diverse beliefs and values rather than simply dismiss these as so many manifestations of error?

Perhaps the most obvious answer is of a pragmatic kind. A theory of human rights is a practical theory; it is a theory about what people should be able to do and what they should not have to suffer. If we are seriously committed to that theory, we shall want it to be practically effective in securing recognition and respect for the rights it identifies as human rights. Indeed, given that the rights at stake are human rights, we shall want it to be practically effective across the entire globe. But, if we have these practical ambitions for our theory, we must take full account of the world we intend it to shape. If that world is one in which people are strongly committed to a variety of beliefs, we must strive to make our theory as compatible as possible with those beliefs. If we do not, people will simply not take up the theory of human rights and, however laudable it may be as a theory, it will remain only a theory.

This reasoning may seem altogether too calculating and worldly to accompany a high-minded commitment to human rights, but there is much to be said for dirtying our hands and achieving something rather than keeping them clean and achieving nothing. But does this pragmatic approach really make room for human diversity within the theory of human rights? It implies that we should operate with two versions of human rights theory: (i) an ideal version that would incorporate the human rights that people really ought to enjoy and that they would indeed enjoy under ideal circumstances and (ii) a modified version of that ideal calculated to win maximum allegiance in the real world. We would begin with our ideal (complete, undefiled and uncompromised) and then trim and temper it until we were left with a modified rump of claims calculated to appeal to as many people as possible. If that is our approach, diversity will certainly have an impact upon what we claim as human rights, but its effect will be external rather than internal to the theory of human rights. Rather than providing a feature of human existence that properly shapes the rights we have, diversity will figure only as an external impediment to the full realisation of human rights and one to which we should make concessions only because we must if we are to make progress in realising human rights. Every such concession will be made grudgingly and only if, on balance, it serves the cause of human rights.

How, then, might diversity figure in a more principled way in our thinking about human rights? How might it find its way into the theory so that it becomes part of the theory rather than just a constraint upon its realisation? The answer is that, instead of regarding diversity of belief and value as a misfortune that obstructs humanity's full enjoyment of its rights, we might regard it as a normal part of the human condition. We might think of it as a natural and unexceptional feature of humanity rather than as an aberration that we should regret. Given the multitude of traditions that people inherit and their own capacity for reflection, it should not be surprising that human beings see the world in different ways and commit themselves to different forms of life. Sometimes that diversity is said to be unique to the modern era though, in truth, there never has been an era during which mankind possessed uniform beliefs and values. Anyway, whatever might be true of the past, what matters is that diversity of belief and value is a feature of humanity now and for the foreseeable future, and it is for now and the foreseeable future that we have to provide. Diversity is for us an essential feature of the human condition and a feature, therefore, that a theory of human rights should not ignore.

Reasonable Disagreement

Philosophers sometimes describe acceptable diversity as 'reasonable disagreement'.[2] Is that a description that we should accept? That is a complex question and I can comment on it here only briefly. It depends, of course, upon what we mean by reasonable and upon the feature of disagreement that we describe as reasonable. If by 'reasonable disagreement' we mean only disagreement for which there is some reason or perhaps good reason (disagreement that is not merely gratuitous), the description seems acceptable enough.

Sometimes the adjective 'reasonable' is linked to 'reason' rather than merely to 'a reason'. Thus, Larmore characterises reasonableness as 'thinking and conversing in good faith and applying, as best one can, the general capacities of reason that belong to every domain of inquiry' (Larmore 1996: 122). Similarly, Rawls describes a plurality of reasonable doctrines as 'the natural outcome of the activities of human reason under enduring free institutions' (Rawls 1993a: xxiv, xvi, 3–4, 36–7, 129, 135, 144). However, if we use 'reason' to give meaning to 'reasonable', we must give it a very generous sense if it is to yield an appropriately inclusive conception of the reasonable. If, for example, we take 'reason' to exclude 'revelation', we shall exclude every kind of religious belief for which revealed knowledge is crucial; yet any endeavour seriously to address human diversity cannot begin by excluding from its purview most of the world's major religions.[3]

If we describe a diversity of belief as reasonable, must that mean that it is made up of beliefs all of which are individually reasonable? Should we understand reasonable disagreement as disagreement arising from conflicting doctrines each of which is independently reasonable as a doctrine? That interpretation of reasonable disagreement will be problematic if we want the parties to the disagreement themselves to accept its reasonableness. One difficulty will be that, in a context of diversity, people will be likely to have different ideas about what constitutes reasonableness, so that the reasonableness of a doctrine will be itself a matter for disagreement. A related difficulty is that it has to be possible for the parties to the disagreement to recognise its reasonableness without jeopardising their own beliefs. There may well be a close limit upon the doctrines that they can recognise as reasonable consistently with the doctrine that that they themselves hold. If I am a Christian, can I find the tenets of Hinduism reasonable? If I am an atheist, can I endorse the reasonableness of the claims of Islam? The only way out of these difficulties would seem to be to adopt a notion of the reasonableness of doctrines that is extremely weak, but, if it is extremely weak, it is not clear what purpose it will serve.

We can understand the notion of reasonable disagreement differently by shifting the focus from doctrines to persons, so that a disagreement will be reasonable in virtue of its being a disagreement among reasonable persons. What constitutes reasonableness in persons? We might answer that question in a way that deprives the shift from doctrines to persons of point. If we identify reasonable persons as persons who hold reasonable doctrines, we shall be no further forward. We can, however, give the reasonableness of persons primacy and insist that we should have regard for people's doctrines because they are doctrines held by reasonable persons, rather than because their doctrines have merit that we can identify independently of their holders. This understanding has the advantage of placing rather greater distance between people and the doctrines of others. That is, I can recognise my disagreement with you as a disagreement with a reasonable person without having to take the further step of endorsing the reasonableness of your particular view. I can therefore avoid the problem of having to endorse as reasonable a view directly contrary to my own.

Moreover, this way of interpreting reasonable disagreement seems much truer to what persuades us (if we are persuaded) to describe the world in this way. It is possible to imagine someone, in complete ignorance of the doctrines that people actually hold, assessing one doctrine after another and finding it to be reasonable or unreasonable. But it would be most surprising if the results of that assessment tallied with the doctrines that actually attract significant support in the world and to which we feel obliged to accord recognition. The reality is surely that we are impressed by the range of doctrines that people actually hold and by the fact that the people who hold them are 'reasonable' in the minimal sense of being sane, sensible and not unduly ignorant. In particular, it is difficult to know how we could identify all of the world's major religions as objects of reasonable disagreement except by reference to the people who subscribe to them. Of course, having noticed the existence of this disagreement, we might search for an explanation in the nature and limits of 'reason'. Rawls's 'burdens of judgement' offer one such explanation (Rawls 1993a: 54–8). But our recognition of disagreement as reasonable still seems one that we arrive at a posteriori rather than a priori. That is, what persuades us to describe as reasonable the large range of very different doctrines that we find in the world is the reasonableness of the people who hold them. It would be disingenuous to pretend that we account those doctrines reasonable because they have passed a test of 'reason' that we have devised independently and in ignorance of the doctrines that people actually hold.

The practical import of accepting that a plurality of beliefs is a normal or reasonable feature of the human condition is that that plurality becomes something that a theory of human rights cannot ignore. Any conception of human rights that overlooks that plurality and supposes that it is something of which humanity either will or should shortly divest itself will be untenable. So both the foundation and the content of a theory of human rights has to be of a kind that makes sense against a background of diversity. But we can ask for more than that; we can also require that it should provide for that diversity. That is, rather than being merely compatible with diversity, we can expect a theory of human rights to tell us something about how we should relate to one another as people with diverse beliefs and values.

Providing For Diversity

If we want a theory of human rights that accommodates and provides for diversity of belief and value, we have to confront two types of question.

(1) How can there be such a theory? The theory of human rights has its own morality and its own content. How can it accommodate other beliefs and values and still survive as a theory in its own right? How can it provide for diversity without either suffering emasculation or becoming embroiled in the very diversity for which it aims to provide?

(2) If we can devise a theory that reconciles human rights with human diversity, how far should we go? How and where should we set the limits of accommodation so that the theory remains a critical theory?

In dealing with these questions, I want to distinguish between two strategies we might adopt in trying to reconcile human rights with human diversity: the continuous and the discontinuous.4§ A continuous strategy would try to establish a continuity between the theory of human rights and the various doctrines to which people are committed. If it is successful, people will be able to recognise that human beings have rights, and to find reason for that recognition, from within their own systems of belief. In that way, the theory of human rights will be 'continuous' with each of the different doctrines that make up the diversity for which it provides. A discontinuous strategy, by contrast, sets out to establish a radical break between the theory of human rights and people's various doctrinal commitments. It deals with diversity by grounding the theory of human rights separately from, and independently of, the different doctrines that make up that diversity. The point of establishing that discontinuity is not to set up a rivalry between the theory of human rights and people's other commitments, but, on the contrary, to enable people to subscribe to both simultaneously.

The Continuous Strategy and Overlapping Consensus

If people hold different and conflicting beliefs, how can there be a continuous strategy? How can people acknowledge a common theory of human rights if they each approach that theory from different and conflicting positions? If a continuous strategy is to be feasible, it needs to discover what Rawls calls an 'overlapping consensus' (Rawls 1993a: 133–72). Different and conflicting doctrines exhibit an overlapping consensus when, despite their different and conflicting contents, there are points at which they agree. An overlapping consensus describes the domain within which doctrines register identical claims even though, outside that domain, they continue to register different and conflicting claims. If we apply that idea to the issue of human rights and human diversity, it suggests that our search for a way of reconciling the two should be a search for an overlapping consensus. We might take all of mankind's different cultures, religious faiths, ideologies, and other systems of belief, and try to find within them a common core of value. If we succeed, we can use that common core to provide the substance of a theory of human rights. We shall then have a theory that avoids conflict with all of the many other doctrines that people hold. Indeed, we shall have a theory that does more than merely avoid conflict; it will enjoy the positive endorsement of all the various doctrines that contribute to the overlapping consensus.

A number of theorists have been attracted by the prospect of founding a theory of human rights upon a global moral consensus. Alan Milne (1986) and Alison Dundes Renteln (1990) are notable examples.[5] The consensual approach is also sometimes implicit in attempts to ground the idea of human rights in a variety of doctrinal positions. Thus, we are presented with the Christian theory of human rights, the Muslim theory of human rights, the Buddhist theory of human rights, the Confucian theory of human rights, the rationalist theory of human rights, and so on. Each of these theories might, of course, turn out to invest human rights with a radically different content, but more commonly they are presented by their proponents in a 'me too' spirit; that is, they are designed to show that these doctrines share a common commitment to human rights.

Despite the obvious attractions of the consensual approach, there are a number of reasons why it is less than satisfactory. I shall document these only briefly. First, and perhaps most obviously, it is doubtful whether there is any value that has been common to every culture and system of belief to which humanity has subscribed at one time or another and in one place or another. Even if we could find values that have been endorsed by everyone everywhere, these are likely to be so meagre, so denuded of content, that they will provide a set of human rights that is hardly worth having. The lowest common denominator is likely to be very low indeed. Cultures and doctrines that ascribe a fundamentally unequal status to different categories of human being are particularly difficult for the consensual approach.

Second, the consensual approach implies a conception of values as modules that are slotted into, and that can be removed without loss from, any system of belief, so that a value remains the same value in whatever system of belief it resides. That ignores the way in which values are not isolable units but intersections in a nexus of moral relations. For example, it matters not just that a moral system recognises something as 'good', but also how it ranks that good in relation to other goods, how it factors that good into people's responsibilities to one another, how it holds that people have, or can come to have, claims to that good, and so on. These considerations are of the first importance if we are trying to uncover values that we can identify as rights.

Third, the consensual strategy threatens to make a theory of human rights superfluous. Why, if its content has to be limited to values already endorsed by all other theories, do we need a theory of human rights? What will it provide that we do not already have? What do we gain if we merely redescribe a pre-existing moral consensus in the language of human rights?

Fourth, what would justify that redescription? A theory of human rights is a particular type of theory: a theory that ascribes certain rights to human individuals in virtue of their humanity. The mere fact that a number of moral theories overlap is no warrant for identifying the domain within which they overlap as the domain of human rights, particularly since some or all of those theories may not themselves identify the values within that domain as human rights. It requires more than an overlapping consensus to generate something that we can describe, with justification, as a theory of human rights.

Fifth, it is not clear what, morally, commends the consensual approach. Certainly, our aim is to find a way of thinking about human rights that takes account of the fact of human diversity. But should our thinking about human rights be subordinated so completely to the demands of other doctrines and ideologies? Should we allow any and every doctrine to exercise a veto over the content of human rights? If our concerns are merely pragmatic, it is easy to see the attractions of the consensual approach. But if we want a theory of human rights that has both moral justification and moral purpose, can it defer so comprehensively to every other moral view that people hold or might hold?

Lastly, and most importantly for the argument I want to develop, the consensual strategy does not so much address diversity as avoid it. We want a theory of rights appropriate to human beings who hold different and conflicting beliefs. Even if the search for an overlapping consensus yields a result, all it will pick out is a portion of value upon which people already agree. There is no reason why we should suppose that that portion of value will be of any help to us when we try to figure out how we should relate to one another as persons with different beliefs and cultures. Suppose, for example, that we discover, among all the systems of value that we scrutinise, agreement that, as far as possible, our basic biological needs should be met and that we should neither inflict upon others, nor ourselves have to endure, unnecessary physical pain. That discovery will be of little help when we try to work out how we should organise a world in which people have different and conflicting beliefs about how they all should live. The search for an overlapping consensus is merely the search for an element of uniformity among diverse systems of belief. It is a search for something other than diversity, rather than a search for a way of dealing with diversity.

The Discontinuous Strategy

An attempt to reconcile human rights and human diversity by way of a continuous strategy seems, then, unlikely to succeed. How would a discontinuous strategy approach that task?

We are supposing that diversity of belief and value is a normal part of the human condition or, at least, a normal part of the human world in which we live and for which we have to provide. Given that state of affairs, we can look to a theory of human rights to provide for that diversity rather than simply to add to it. That is, we might conceive the theory of human rights as a having a different purpose from the various other doctrines we find in the world. People will continue to disagree about the ends to which we should commit our lives, about whether there is a God and, if so, about what He requires of us, about whether, if there is no God, there are still standards by which we should live and, if so, what those standards are and upon what they are grounded, and so on. The task of a theory of human rights is not to add yet another voice to that cacophony of disagreement. Its task is to provide for a world in which there is that disagreement. But it is to provide for that world not by itself entering the lists of doctrinal controversy and attempting to declare which doctrine is true and which false. That is not its business. Instead, it should be concerned with how people ought to relate to one another as people with different beliefs. So its proper concern is with people who hold doctrines, rather than with the doctrines that they hold.

We might, therefore, assign a theory of human rights a role quite different from that of other doctrines. We might model its different role by allowing for different 'levels' of concern and by presenting the theory of human rights as a theory whose concerns lie at a different level from those of other doctrines. If we think of doctrines in general, and the disagreements to which they give rise, as constituting a first level of concern, we can think of a theory of human rights (of the sort we are now considering) as functioning at a second level. A theory of human rights neither addresses the issues nor participates in the debates that occur at the first level. It does not set out to compete with other doctrines in that way. Rather, accepting the fact of first-level disagreement, it tells us how individuals should relate to one another as individuals who are caught up in first-level disagreement. In that sense, its concerns lie at a second level. That is also the way in which a theory of human rights can be 'discontinuous' with other doctrines. It places itself outside and above the arena of doctrinal disagreement and seeks only to regulate people's relations with one another given that they have to live in that arena of disagreement.

Of course, if a theory of human rights is to be genuinely discontinuous with the disagreement it seeks to regulate, it must be independent of the doctrines that contribute to that disagreement. It must be what Rawls calls a 'freestanding' theory (Rawls 1993a: 12–13). If it does not have that free-standing character, it will simply be dragged into first-level disagreement and the parties to that disagreement will have no reason to regard it as an independent theory that stands outside and above their doctrinal disputes and to which they must subordinate the demands of their doctrines. So, for example, in a society populated by Christians, Muslims and Hindus, it will not do to proffer a specifically Christian or Muslim or Hindu theory of human rights, since any such theory would be party to the doctrinal disputes that divide the society. If a theory of human rights is to regulate in a second-level way the lives of people in a multi-faith society, it must be independent of the different faiths present in that society.

The theory of human rights seems well equipped to perform that task since it is pre-eminently a theory about the status of human persons. Equal rights presuppose equal standing so that a theory that ascribes the same fundamental rights to human persons must be one that ascribes equal moral standing to persons. What people have a right to is what they are owed, so a theory of human rights is a theory of what people are owed merely in virtue of being human. Set in the context of a world in which people have different and conflicting beliefs about how they should live, it most readily issues in the prescription that each person should be free to live according to his or her beliefs. If we allowed one person to impose his beliefs upon another, we should be either according greater standing to the person who imposes than to the person who is imposed upon, or not taking seriously the idea of reasonable disagreement. Of course, each person's freedom will be constrained by every other person's freedom so that people's freedom to live according to their beliefs will not be unlimited. But the limits that people come up against will be limits imposed by their equal status as persons and not limits grounded in an evaluation of the different merits of their different doctrines.

None of this is intended to imply that the theory of human rights must be or can be entirely free of controversy. On the contrary, I shall indicate, in a moment, the sorts of controversy to which it remains subject. But the fact that the theory is primarily a theory about the status of personhood does mean that it is well suited to playing a second-level role in a context of disagreement. It enables us to set out the rights that people should enjoy in a context of diversity independently of the doctrines that make up that diversity.

It is that separation of people from doctrines that leads discontinuity theorists to claim 'neutrality' or 'impartiality' for the way in which they provide for doctrinal diversity. Claims to impartiality or neutrality have proved peculiarly provocative, often because those who respond adversely to them ignore (sometimes, it seems, wilfully) the limited character of the neutrality or impartiality that is the subject of those claims. The theory of human rights that I am setting out here is neutral with respect to different doctrines only in that it does not aspire to evaluate them, but simply to provide for their holders on some ground other than the alleged merits or demerits of their doctrines. In other words, its neutrality resides only in its discontinuity. It does not claim to be neutral with respect to every normative issue – how could any prescriptive theory be comprehensively neutral? Nor, as I shall indicate in due course, is there only one way of dealing with diversity that can claim to do so impartially (see also Jones 1998). Nor, again, need a discontinuous conception of human rights be neutral in its consequences for different doctrines. Suppose one doctrine requires its adherents to impose itself upon non-believers, while another requires its adherents to abstain from any such behaviour. Under the sort of human rights arrangement we are contemplating, the first doctrine will find itself frustrated in a way that the second will not. But that will not show that the theory has betrayed its second-level nature and adopted a first-level view of the relative merits of the two doctrines. Its different impact upon the two doctrines is a merely the incidental consequence of its being impartial among the people who hold them.

The nature of this role explains why a theory of human rights must enjoy a special status relative to other doctrines. It should have priority over other doctrines in that it should set the terms upon which people are able to act on their beliefs. What justifies its priority is not a claim to epistemological superiority; it does not claim to be 'truer' or 'better' than other doctrines and rightfully to take precedence over them for that reason. It is simply that it functions at a different level from them. It aims to regulate relations between people who hold doctrines and it could not perform that role if it were subordinated to, or placed in competition with, the doctrines that they hold. So the special status that we should claim for a theory of human rights stems neither from arrogant presumption nor from insensitivity to other beliefs; it derives simply from the regulative (second-level) nature of the theory.

If we adhere to a particular system of belief, but are also to embrace this theory of human rights, we shall have to look upon the world from two different vantage points. As adherents of a particular system of belief, we shall see the world as it appears from within our particular system of belief. But, as adherents of a second-level conception of human rights, we must also view the world from a vantage point external to our particular system of belief. That is, we must see the world as populated by people with different and conflicting systems of belief of which our own is merely one. We must appreciate that other people have reasons for believing what they do, just as we have reasons for believing what we do, and that others' beliefs matter to them as ours do to us. We are then in a position to appreciate that the world should be one in which we are each able to live according to our own beliefs, even though we continue to hold that our own beliefs are correct and that others' contrary beliefs are mistaken. Adopting a perspective external to our particular system of belief does not require us to shelve that system of belief. It does not require that we substitute a belief in human rights for whatever other beliefs we might hold. Clearly, if it did, it would defeat the whole point of having a second-level theory of human rights. It requires only that we hold our beliefs with an appropriate awareness that others are committed to their beliefs as we are to our own. We must therefore see the world from both perspectives rather than from only one.

For some people, the world may appear pretty much the same from both perspectives. In other words, the injunctions of their particular system of belief may be the same as, or at least not in conflict with, the demands of human rights. In the society for which Rawls provides in his *Political Liberalism*, he anticipates that the different comprehensive doctrines held by its members will come to overlap in supporting the political conception of justice that he develops for that society. Thus, the conception of justice that he develops in the first instance as a discontinuous and free-standing view is one that he hopes will come to be endorsed by his citizens' different comprehensive doctrines. If his hope is realised, his citizens will experience a continuity of commitment from their different comprehensive doctrines to their shared conception of justice. Analogously, we may hope that people's different and conflicting doctrines will converge in supporting a second-level theory of human rights. But that is not a hope upon which we should rely. There need be no overlapping consensus among different and competing doctrines and, even if there is, it need not coincide with a theory of human rights. As I have previously argued, a theory of human rights should not presuppose nor should it depend upon the existence of an overlapping consensus among different systems of belief. Indeed, a second-level theory of human rights will be needed all the more, and will be all the more significant in implication, in the absence of an overlapping consensus.[6]

Second-Level Issues

If a theory of human rights can claim to regulate, rather than to compete or conflict with, first-level doctrines, it is a different matter when it comes up against other second-level theories. Since these compete for the same moral space as the theory of human rights, that theory cannot respond to them in the same detached way that it deals with first-level disputes among doctrines. From the perspective of a human rights theory, issues that arise at the second level divide into two sorts: (a) issues that are 'external' to the theory in that they arise from challenges presented by alternatives to the human rights approach, and (b) issues that are 'internal' in that they arise within the theory of human rights itself. I look at each in turn.

External Issues

A theory of human rights is not the only sort of second-level position from which we might seek to deal with diversity of belief and value. We might follow the lead of Thomas Hobbes and turn to a collective decision procedure for a second-level solution. That is, rather than construct an order in which we give equal freedom to each individual to live according to his own beliefs, we might subject everyone's beliefs to the decision of a common authority (which could be an authority of any kind, including the most direct of democracies) and require everyone to conform with whatever that authority decrees. There are very many reasons why we should hesitate to do things in that way, but this sort of Hobbesian solution qualifies as a discontinuous strategy provided that it is grounded (as it was for Hobbes) upon something other than a claim that the belief or the value selected by the sovereign authority must be the true belief or the correct value.

Alternatively, a second-level theory might spurn a collective solution and retain the sort of distributive approach we find in a theory of human rights, but dissent from another of its features. It might, for example, accord a fundamentally unequal status to different categories of human being. Since my concern in this paper is to investigate how a theory of human rights might take account of diversity, rather than to justify the very idea of human rights, I shall not stop to defend it against these alternatives. My main concern here is simply to concede that the conception of human rights I have set out in this paper is not the only kind of split-level approach there can be and that a theory of human rights has to compete with, rather than stand aloof from, other forms of that approach. However, I do want to comment upon one way in which the human rights approach is frequently challenged since it is of particular relevance to the issues raised by diversity of belief and value.

Human rights thinking is often said to be individualistic. That observation is correct in so far as the unit of moral standing in a theory of human rights must be the individual person. But that is the only way in which it need be individualistic. The idea of human rights is not wedded to a belief that a good life must be individualistic in form. On the contrary, the attribution of equal moral standing to individual persons is entirely consistent with a conception of the best life as non-individualistic. The theory of human rights does, of course, place limits upon what may be done to create or preserve a collective form of life; individuals may not be coerced into becoming or remaining members of a community or an association. That, in turn, may be said to make collective forms of life more difficult to sustain than individualist forms. But, if a theory of human rights has that effect (and it is not clear that it must), that will be a consequence of the moral standing it accords to each individual and not of its being committed to the superiority of a particular form of life. Identifying a form of life as good and setting the terms upon which that life may be pursued are two separate exercises.

Even if we accept that, however, we may still feel that the theory of human rights is unduly limiting if the only rights it can recognise are rights that might be held by individual persons. Some of the goods that play a significant role in people's lives are collective in nature and it seems implausible to suppose that individuals might have rights, *qua* individuals, to those collective goods.[7] If there are rights to collective goods, it would seem that those must be group rights and it is a common criticism of theories of human rights that they do not, and cannot, recognise groups as possessors of rights.

In the present context, that criticism arises most frequently where a system of belief forms part of a culture. Cultures are necessarily collective in nature; they constitute shared systems of belief and shared forms of life. A belief might be unique to an individual or it might be held by an individual quite independently of the fact that the same belief is held by other people; but that could not be true if the belief formed part of a culture. A culture is necessarily a group phenomenon. Thus, if a culture is important to the well-being of those whose culture it is, it will be a good that is collective to the cultural group; and, if that culture is to be an object of rights, it would seem that those must be rights held by the group *qua* group rather than by its members severally. Consequently, if part of the diversity for which we attempt to provide through a split-level approach is cultural diversity, we may seem stymied if we have to regard individual human beings rather than groups as the bearers of rights.

Can a theory of human rights overcome this apparent difficulty? Can it find a place for group rights? The answer depends upon what we understand a group right to be. We may interpret group rights either as 'corporate' rights or as 'collective' rights. I use these as terms to which I attach my own meanings. If we understand a group right as a corporate right, we shall understand it as a right held by a group that has independent moral standing as a group. We shall accord the group an identity and a status that, morally, does not reduce to the several identities and statuses of its individual members. The group will enjoy the same sort of independent and irreducible standing as a right-holding person. If, for example, that is how we understand a cultural group's right of self-determination, we shall ascribe standing to the cultural group *qua* group and we shall conceive its rights as rights held and wielded by the group as a corporate entity, rather than simply as rights held in some way by the individuals who make up the group at any particular moment. Understood according to this corporate model, group rights will fall outside the compass of human rights since they will be rights borne by corporate entities rather than by human persons, and they will be grounded in whatever gives those corporate entities their moral standing, rather than merely in the claims of humanity or personhood.

If, however, we conceive a group right as a collective right, we shall conceive it quite differently. A group right assumes a collective form if we conceive it as a right held jointly by the individuals who make up the group. For example, I, as a single individual, may have a claim to a particular collective good, but that claim, taken on its own, may be insufficient to give me a right to the good. The same may be true of the claim, taken singly, of each other individual who has a stake in the collective good. If, however, we take all of these individuals and treat their several claims as a joint claim, that may well make the case for their having a joint or 'collective' right to the good. A collective right is properly described as a group right since it is a right that the members of the group hold as a group and that none of them holds as an independent individual. But, in contrast to the corporate conception, the collective conception does not require that we ascribe moral standing to the group independently of its members. On the contrary, the moral standing required for the group's right is provided by the standing of its several members, rather than by the group as an independent moral entity.[8]

Consider again the specific case of cultural rights. Suppose we have a body of people who form a cultural minority and who, for all the usual reasons, have an interest in the continuance of their culture, but who find their culture in danger of being overwhelmed by that of the majority society. The interest of any single member of the minority in the maintenance of his culture is unlikely to be adequate to justify imposing duties upon the majority society to institute measures to protect and sustain the culture of the minority. But the joint interest of all the individuals who make up the cultural minority in the maintenance of their culture may well suffice, in which case the members of the cultural minority will possess a right jointly that none of them possesses individually. So, in that way, we can ascribe a right to a group of individuals as a group even though we invest the group with no moral standing that is not reducible to the independent moral standing of its individual members. That alone is not enough to show that these collective cultural rights are human rights, since there are additional tests that they have to pass if they are to be human rights. But since collective rights, unlike corporate rights, need appeal only to the moral standing of individual persons, they constitute group rights of a sort that a theory of human rights might accommodate.[9]

If the split-level approach that I am proposing throws up questions about the relevant unit of standing to which it does not itself provide the answers, might that indicate that I have the content of the two levels precisely the wrong way round? Rather than dealing with cultural diversity by way of units of standing, perhaps we should arbitrate among different possible units of standing by way of cultures. It will then be cultures that perform a second-level role in relation to competing views about the relevant unit of standing. Each culture will determine for its own population what the unit of standing is to be – individuals or groups and, if groups, which groups.

There are two reasons why this inversion of the content that I have given the split-level approach cannot be satisfactory. One is practical. Disagreements arise within cultures as well as between them and, when we are faced with that sort of dissensus, the issue of standing is thrown back at us: *we* have to decide whose voice is to count and to whose voice we should listen. The other is more theoretical. Can we give moral ultimacy to a culture, as though a culture were itself something possessed of moral standing? Giving ultimate moral standing to a culture, as opposed its bearers, would be rather like giving moral standing to a language or a painting or a musical composition. We may value these things, but we do not normally do so by ascribing them an independent moral standing analogous to the standing we ascribe to human persons or human groups. If cultures matter morally, it is because they matter to and for people and, if that is so, the issue of how people are to count morally must precede rather than follow our encounter with cultures.

Internal Issues

We cannot, then, treat disputes over whether human beings have rights as first-level disputes for which a theory of human rights can perform the role of second-level arbiter. Those disputes belong to the second level and a theory of human rights is necessarily a party to them. Rather than refereeing a contest in which it takes no part, it must be itself a participant in the contest. That does not mean, of course, that we cannot continue to insist that the human rights approach is the right one. But in insisting upon that approach, we shall be rejecting, rather than regulating, theories that challenge the fundamentals of human rights.[10]

It is not only theories that challenge human rights that raise second-level issues. Those issues may arise even if we limit ourselves to the idea of human rights, since that idea and its implications are open to different interpretations. For example, I have suggested that, faced with first-level differences in belief, a theory of human rights should extend equal freedom to people to live according to their beliefs. However, that proposal may leave room for different possibilities in how precisely we define each person's domain of equal freedom. Many of those who found themselves on different sides in the Rushdie Affair were not in dispute over whether people should enjoy freedom of belief; they disagreed only over the proper make-up of each person's domain of freedom.

Similarly, disputes over who is to count as 'human' for purposes of human rights is a question that belongs to the second level. Imagine there are four adult individuals, A, B, C and D, who disagree over whether D is a person and therefore over whether D has the rights that normally accompany personhood. A and B think D is not a person; C and D himself think D is a person. D might, for example, be black; A and B might be white racists; and C might be white, but not a racist. It is fairly obvious that this is not the sort of dispute that we can deal with satisfactorily by turning to a second-level theory of human rights. We proposed dealing with doctrinal disputes about how we should live by retreating from doctrines to persons and by assigning each person a right to live according to his own beliefs. But we cannot similarly deal with a dispute about personhood by retreating to an idea of personhood because that is what is in dispute. If we tried to make that move, how would we decide whether D should or should not figure at the higher level without simultaneously entering into the lower level dispute about D's personhood? Furthermore, how could we arrive at any higher level conclusion that made sense? If we concluded that each person should be free to live according to his own conception of who was a person, A and B might be adjudged free to enslave D since they believe D to be a non-person, while C and D would be free to resist D's enslavement since they believe D to be a person.

All of that is plain enough. In the past, questions of who should count as a person have been real issues; nowadays, we rightly give short shrift to suggestions that we might limit the range of 'personhood' or 'humanity' on grounds of race or class or caste. But some variations on this issue are less straightforward. Consider the case of abortion. We might suppose that abortion is a classic example of an issue that we should deal with at arm's length. People differ radically in their views on abortion, so perhaps a theory of human rights should declare itself neither for nor against abortion, but, instead, should stand aloof from the issue and prescribe only that each person should be free to act according to his or her beliefs on abortion. That is certainly what many people, including many politicians, think is the right arrangement given the unresolvable nature of disagreements about abortion in our world.

We might, however, conceive abortion as an issue within the idea of human rights, rather than one that is settled by that idea. Should a foetus count as a human being for right-holding purposes?[11] If we believe it should, we shall include it in the community of moral beings and exclude it from the class of beings that we may dispose of at will. If, on the other hand, we give the foetus no moral status, we shall be happy to ascribe people the right to practise abortion as they themselves judge fit.[12] In other words, if we locate the issue of abortion within the theory of human rights, it will be a second-level issue, and if we permit people to engage in abortion, we shall be taking a stand, rather than no stand, on that second-level issue.

That is not to say that something like a split-level approach to the issue of abortion is not possible. If we are prepared, at the second level, to treat articulate participants in the dispute about abortion as the only claimants that count, we can respond to that dispute by allowing those articulate participants to engage in abortion, or not, according to their different convictions. But in adopting that strategy, we shall have already decided that it is acceptable that the fate of a foetus should depend upon the different beliefs of different people and that the foetus itself has no moral status that vetoes its disposal by those people. In other words, we shall have already taken sides on the issue that is fundamental to disputes about abortion.[13] We could respond to disagreements about infanticide in a directly parallel fashion: rather than confronting that issue head on, we might give parents the freedom to dispose or not to dispose of their infant children as their own beliefs dictate. Why do we not do that? Because, in the case of infanticide, almost everyone accepts that infants have independent moral standing and that, consequently, it is entirely unacceptable that their lives should be placed at the mercy of their parents' beliefs.

Thus, the two-level approach to human rights that I have been defending does not provide for cases in which the dispute is about who should count as a human being with rights. Indeed, we might extend that limitation beyond the domain of human rights. Proponents of animal rights might similarly insist that animals should not be placed at the mercy of human beliefs and wishes and, consequently, that a society that allows people to choose between eating or not eating, using or not using, animals cannot claim to remain neutral on the issue of animal rights. My point in making these remarks is not to argue either against abortion or for animal rights; it is simply to acknowledge the limits of a two-level approach. That approach provides for differences of belief among the members of the moral community about how they should conduct their lives; it does not provide for disputes about who should count as a member of the moral community. Whatever the merits of the two-level approach as a way of dealing with disagreement, it should not allow us to take for granted that only the articulate have rights.

Conclusion

The understanding of human rights that I have presented in this article does not, then, provide an easy solution to every sort of disagreement. It places human rights outside and above some disputes and it enables human rights to respond to those disputes impartially. But it does not extricate human rights from every form of controversy. That need not occasion disappointment. If we could have a moral theory that retreated from, rather than faced up to, fundamental issues concerning the moral status of human beings, would we want it?

In spite of its limits, the two-level approach does, I believe, offer a way of dealing with diversity that has very considerable range. Indeed, if we think a theory of human rights should take seriously and should accommodate the diversity of belief and culture in our world, rather than respond to these as if they were of no consequence, it is difficult to see how it might do that without pursuing a discontinuous strategy.

I do not claim that my account provides comprehensively for human rights. I have considered only how our thinking on human rights might approach the subject of diversity of belief and value. In other areas, human rights will need other arguments. As I have argued elsewhere (Jones 1994: 117–9), the search for a single grand theory of human rights may be misplaced; different rights may be sustained by different reasons.

NOTES

1. For sceptical views of human rights that relate in various ways to diversity of belief and value, see Brown (1997), MacIntyre (1985: 66–71), Nelson (1990), and Pollis and Schwab (1979). For an equally sceptical view that, nevertheless, holds on to the idea of human rights, see Rorty (1993).
2. See Rawls (1993a: especially Lecture II), Larmore (1987: Ch.3; 1996: Ch.7), and Barry (1995: Ch.7). Although my general approach in this paper is heavily indebted to the work of John Rawls, the account of human rights that I develop is fundamentally different from his. For Rawls's own account, see Rawls (1993b). For a

critical examination of Rawls's attempt to provide for human rights by way of his political conception of international justice, see Jones (1996).
3. In fact, neither Rawls nor Larmore excludes religious faith from reasonable belief.
4. I borrow these terms from Ronald Dworkin (1990: 16–22).
5. Renteln proposes an anthropological approach that would search empirically for a minimum moral consensus. Milne's approach is more philosophical. He sets out a minimum morality that, he argues, is necessary for social life as such and is therefore to be found among all cultures and civilisations. However, he does not rely solely upon that common morality for his account of human rights since he is able to make the transition from that morality to universal human rights only by invoking Kant's humanity principle: 'Treat humanity, whether in your own person or in that of another, always as an end withal and never merely as a means.' Although I use Rawls's term 'overlapping consensus' to describe the domain of pre-existing cultural agreement contemplated by Renteln and Milne, Rawls himself uses the notion of overlapping consensus to describe a rather different possibility. See note 6.
6. Abdullahi A. An-Na'im (1990a; 1992) argues that a cross-cultural consensus on human rights is not something that we can expect simply to discover, but something that we should work to construct. Significantly, Rawls himself does not suppose that an overlapping consensus is something that lies dormant in a variety of comprehensive doctrines just waiting to be discovered. Rather, his hope is that his political conception of justice will provide a focus around which an overlapping consensus can form. That is why his political conception of justice needs, at least in the first instance, its own independent foundation. (Rawls cites An-Na'im's work (1990b), reinterpreting Islam in a form that is consistent with constitutional democracy, as a 'perfect example' of overlapping consensus (Rawls 1997: 782–3).) Analogously, the conception of human rights I am proposing here is not something we should expect to find ready-made within all or most systems of belief, even though we might hope that people will find a way of making their systems of belief 'congruent with, or supportive of, or else not in conflict with' (Rawls 1993a: 140) that conception.
7. In fact, there are collective goods that might plausibly be the objects of individual rights. See Réaume (1998).
8. I model what I say here on the conception of collective rights proposed by Joseph Raz (1986: 207–8). The claim about the moral standing required for a collective right is my own, but it is also implicit in Raz's account.
9. I examine more fully the significance of the difference between these two conceptions of group rights in Jones (1999a; 1999b).
10. To avoid undue complication, I have developed my argument as if doctrines or theories had either first-level or second-level concerns. In reality, a major system of belief (such as, for example, a religion) may address both. In that case, a second-level theory of human rights may stand in a regulative non-rival relation to the first-level components of a system of belief, but in a competitive non-regulative relation to its second-level components (although, of course, it is quite possible that the second-level aspects of a system of belief may complement, rather than conflict with, human rights thinking).
11. I have previously spoken of human 'persons' and, of course, a foetus does not possess the qualities normally associated with 'personhood'. However, I assume that we can intelligibly ascribe rights to human beings that are not 'persons', even though there are some human rights that we can intelligibly ascribe only to persons (for example, rights to freedom of belief and to political participation).
12. The debate about abortion is, of course, much more complex than this, but that does not, I think, affect the general point I am making here about the limits of a two-level approach.

13. Compare Michael Sandel's use of the cases of abortion and slavery in his critique of 'minimalist liberalism' (Sandel 1996: 19–24).

REFERENCES

An-Na'im, A.A., 1990a. Problems of universal cultural legitimacy for human rights. In *Human Rights in Africa: Cross-Cultural Perspectives*, ed. An-Na'im, A.A. and Deng, F.M. Washington, The Brookings Institution.
    1990b, *Toward an Islamic Reformation: Civil Liberties, Human Rights, and International Law*. Syracuse: Syracuse University Press.
    1992. Toward a cross-cultural approach to defining international standards of human rights. In *Human Rights in Cross-Cultural Perspectives*, ed. An-Na'im, A.A. Philadelphia, University of Pennsylvania Press.
Barry, B. 1995, Justice as Impartiality. Oxford: Oxford University Press.
Brown, C. 1997. Universal human rights: a critique. *International Journal of Human Rights*, Vol.1, No.1, pp.41–65.
Dworkin, R., 1990. Foundations of liberal equality. In *The Tanner Lectures on Human Values, XI, 1990*, ed. Peterson, G.B. Salt Lake City, University of Utah Press.
Jones, P. 1994, *Rights*. Basingstoke: Macmillan.
    1996. International human rights: philosophical or political? In *National Rights, International Obligations*, ed. Caney, S., George, D. and Jones, P. Boulder (CO), Westview Press.
    1998. Political theory and cultural diversity. *Contemporary Review of International, Social and Political Philosophy*, Vol.1, No.1, pp.28–62.
    1999a. Human rights, group rights and peoples' rights. *Human Rights Quarterly*, Vol.21, No.1, pp.80–107.
    1999b. Group rights and group oppression. *Journal of Political Philosophy*, Vol.7, No.4, pp.353–77.
Larmore, C. 1987, *Patterns of Moral Complexity*. Cambridge: Cambridge University Press.
    1996, *The Morals of Modernity*. Cambridge: Cambridge University Press.
MacIntyre, A. 1985, *After Virtue*, second edition. London: Duckworth.
Milne, A.J.M. 1986, *Human Rights and Human Diversity*. Basingstoke: Macmillan.
Nelson, J.O. 1990. Against human rights. *Philosophy*, Vol.65, pp.341–8.
Pollis, A. and Schwab, P., 1979. Human rights: a western construct with limited applicability. In *Human Rights: Cultural and Ideological Perspectives*, ed. Pollis, A. and Schwab, P. New York, Praeger.
Rawls, J. 1993a, *Political Liberalism*. New York: Columbia University Press.
    1993b. The law of peoples. In *On Human Rights: the Oxford Amnesty Lectures 1993*, ed. Shute, S. and Hurley, S. New York, Basic Books.
    1997. The idea of public reason revisited. *University of Chicago Law Review*, Vol.64, pp.765–807.
Raz, J. 1986, *The Morality of Freedom*. Oxford: Clarendon Press.
Réaume, D.G. 1988. Individuals, groups, and rights to public goods. *University of Toronto Law Journal*, Vol.38, No.1, pp.1–27.
Renteln, A.D. 1990, *International Human Rights: Universalism versus Relativism*. Newbury Park (CA): Sage.
Rorty, R., 1993. Human rights, rationality, and sentimentality. In *On Human Rights: the Oxford Amnesty Lectures 1993*, ed. Shute, S. and Hurley, S. New York, Basic Books.
Sandel, M. 1996, *Democracy's Discontent: America in Search of a Public Philosophy*. Cambridge (MA): Belknap.

4

Human Rights, Compatibility and Diverse Cultures

SIMON CANEY

Many are critical of human rights, arguing that they are a distinctively western concept and have little or no application in non-western contexts. To pursue human rights, it is frequently asserted, is to be intolerant of non-western practices and forms of life. The latter, the argument runs, are incompatible with the pursuit of human rights and for this reason human rights should be abandoned. These assertions are commonplace. To take just one example, Danilo Zolo maintains in his work *Cosmopolis* that rights are the heirs of the 'Judaeo-Christian tradition' (Zolo 1997: 61).[1] Furthermore, he describes rights simply as a feature of westernisation (Zolo 1997: 118–20). He concludes that 'The universal character of "human rights" is therefore a rationalistic postulate not only without substantiation in the theoretical sphere but also historically contested by cultures different from western culture.' (Zolo 1997: 118.) This empirical claim is widespread, as is the inference from it that human rights have no place in non-western societies.

This paper examines several issues surrounding the relationship between human rights and non-western cultural practices. In particular, it pursues three aims. First, it provides an account of the various ways in which human rights may be compatible or incompatible with non-western ethical ideals. It challenges the prevailing dualistic assumption that an ethical tradition either affirms human rights or is antagonistic toward them. Second, it addresses the question of whether it matters if human rights are incompatible with

This article was completed during my tenure of a Leverhulme Research Fellowship. I am grateful to the Leverhulme Trust for its support.

ethical ideals, arguing that there is a powerful prima-facie case for exploring the possibility of reconciliation between human rights and other moral values. Lastly, it explores the relationship between human rights and one specific non-western ethical tradition, Theravada Buddhism, arguing that the latter provides an interesting counter-example to the dogma that all non-western ethical traditions are hostile to human rights. The prevailing assumption that all non-western value-systems are incompatible with egalitarian liberal ideals is, therefore, shown to be too sweeping and undiscriminating. In short, this paper examines how human rights may relate to non-western moral ideals, why this relationship matters, and applies it to one case study.

Prior to developing these points, it should be made clear that I am not disputing the historical contention that the concepts of 'rights' in general and 'human rights' in particular arose in the west. These claims strike me as credible ones. It is important to note, however, that this historical claim about the source of the idea does not entail that human rights are now inappropriate in other parts of the world or are not or would not be affirmed there. That one idea arose in one society at one time does not establish that it has no applicability in other societies at other times (Donnelly 1989: 60).

The Nature of the Relationship between Rights and Ethical Traditions

Let us begin, then, by exploring the various ways in which human rights may relate to ethical traditions. Before we do this, however, we should record that identifying an individual ethical tradition is highly difficult and subject to controversy. By a tradition, I mean a body of thought and doctrine comprising a shared set of values, beliefs and modes of reasoning. Thus defined, it is clear that identifying a tradition is far from straightforward. Should one, for example, refer to Christianity or to subcategories such as Anglicanism, Methodism, Presbyterianism and Congregationalism as traditions? Any answer to this question would, I suggest, take into account whether the putative tradition has an integrated and coherent body of doctrine which is distinct from others and whether the adherents to these doctrines perceive themselves and their doctrines to form a distinct approach or be part of a larger school of thought. Applying these criteria requires sensitivity, judgement and an awareness of the vagueness and disputed nature of the boundaries of traditions. Bearing this in mind, we may now turn to the ways in which human rights may relate to ethical traditions.

Those who criticise human rights by arguing that they are incompatible with some ethical traditions tend to operate with a dualistic framework, according to which a tradition either affirms a commitment to human rights or it does not and is, therefore, incompatible with human rights. This binary approach is, however, too simplistic to be of much use. We can see this by distinguishing between (at least) seven logical, possible relations between human rights (HRs) and ethical traditions (ETs).

1. *Incompatibility*: HRs are incompatible with an ET when they prescribe incompatible actions. To give one example, HRs are often said to be incompatible with various aspects of Islam, notably its treatment of women or those who renounce Islam (although there is considerable controversy about whether these are defining features of Islam (Mayer 1994)).

2. *Compatibility*: HRs are compatible with an ET when the actions they prescribe do not conflict. Compatibility, thus, obtains when an ET enjoins people to act in certain ways (be kind, merciful, humble and polite, say), none of which are inconsistent with the behaviour required by a human rights regime. Compatibility occurs when HRs can peacefully coexist with an ET.

3. *Convergence*: HRs and an ET converge when they prescribe the same actions, but do so for different reasons. Convergence, thus, occurs when HRs and an ET (or number of ETs) are not only consistent: they actually recommend the same actions, but they do so drawing on different concepts and ideals. To illustrate: many ethical traditions do not invoke the concept of rights, emphasising instead the duties of rulers or the character traits of a virtuous ruler. They adopt, that is, a duty-based or virtue-based approach. They may nonetheless converge on some political principles. Whereas a human rights theorist will argue that people have a right not to be murdered or tortured or treated cruelly, these other approaches may yield the same moral conclusions but give different reasons, not invoking rights but arguing instead that rulers have duties to their subjects not to maltreat them. Consider another example: many western liberals defend democracy on individualistic grounds. Some defend it on the grounds that people

have a right to shape political decisions and others defend it on the grounds that it best protects people's rights. As Daniel Bell has pointed out, however, one can give a non-individualistic defence of democracy, which draws on values that appeal to communitarian east-Asian ethical traditions such as Confucianism. Rather than invoke the entitlements of individuals, this communitarian argument maintains that democratic institutions are valuable because they foster and strengthen associations and communities (Bell 1995: 36–40). Invoking such considerations, he is critical of authoritarian non-democratic modes of decision-making, such as that practised by Lee Kwan Yew of Singapore, on the grounds that 'authoritarianism undermines patriotism' (Bell 1997: 10–16). Democracy combined with freedom of association will, he maintains, generate patriotism. These examples, thus, illustrate the central point that different arguments can be given for the same institutions and the same principles.

The concept of convergence, it should be noted, corresponds to Rawls's concept of an 'overlapping consensus' (Rawls 1993: 133–72). He employs this term in his treatment of domestic politics, where he argues that the different comprehensive doctrines that exist in a liberal political system will all converge in support for the values of political liberalism, each providing their own distinctive justifications for those liberal values. Now, Nigel Dower and Charles Taylor have both drawn on Rawls's concept and have defended the possibility of a global overlapping consensus (Dower 1998: 12–13, 43; Taylor 1999: 124–6, 133–8, 143–4).[2] This strategy has also been developed and applied by the Muslim scholar Abdullahi An-Na'im (1992a: 2–6; 1992b: 28–9; 1999: 153, 166–8) and by Joseph Chan (1999: 212).

This idea has a great deal of plausibility and application. It both recognises the radical diversity of views and also does not make the mistake of thinking that this precludes agreement. We should, however, note that it suffers from one problem not experienced by Rawls's domestic use of the concept of an 'overlapping consensus'. One of the central features of Rawls's account of an overlapping consensus is his explanation of how it can come about and he outlines the political factors (including a shared political system) that help to bring it into existence (Rawls 1993: 133–72, especially 158–68). The problem with the idea of a global overlapping consensus is that these factors (such as a shared political system with its dynamics encouraging convergence) are absent at the global level. A global overlapping consensus is, therefore, that more difficult to attain.

4. Identity$_i$: HRs and an ET can be described as identical$_i$ either (a) when they affirm the same fundamental value or values, or (b) when they affirm the same values and give the same kind of reasoning in support of them. Identity$_i$, thus, refers to cases in which adherents to HRs and adherents to an ET prescribe the same action. Unlike the previous relationship (namely, convergence), however, they do not endorse the same value for different reasons. Rather, (4) obtains either when neither ETs nor HRs affirm any further reason for their value (it is just a basic value for them) or when they do, but give the same reasoning.

Consider 4(a). Many have argued that there is agreement in all cultures on some fundamental moral values.[3] Murder, cruelty, lying, betrayal, drought and famine are, for example, universally deemed to be wrong and Christians, Muslims, Buddhists, Sikhs, Hindus and atheists, for example, do not disagree on these matters.[4] Others have added that all ethical traditions maintain that you should treat others as you would want them to treat you. This 'golden rule' is, for example, affirmed by Christianity, Judaism, Islam, Buddhism, Sikhism and Confucianism (Hick 1989: 316–26; Kung 1997: 97–9, 110). There is, in addition to this, cross-cultural agreement on other values, for example, people's duties to their friends and families. Such virtues are, of course, central to Confucianism and to many African traditions (Gyeke 1997: 35–76), but they are, of course, ones also strongly emphasised by western traditions and a thoroughly agent-neutral morality which requires us to treat strangers as we would loved ones is utterly alien to western traditions. There is, thus, considerable convergence on certain fundamental moral beliefs.[5]

Consider also 4(b). This applies when HRs and ETs affirm the same conclusions and give the same reasons. To illustrate, Aristotle argues in *The Politics* that a system of common ownership leads to strife (because people cannot agree on who can use which common resources and when). In addition, it is inefficient and efficiency would be enhanced under a system of private ownership because each property owner has an incentive to look after their resources (Aristotle 1986: II, 5, especially 1263a21). Now, setting aside the question of whether these considerations are telling, it is quite clear that these considerations have been and, in fact, are adduced by members of contemporary liberal democracies to defend the right to private ownership. In other words, the same reasons are given for the same conclusions by people of radically different contexts.

Recognising common values does not, one should note, entail agreement on how those values should be ranked. Indeed, many who argue that there are cross-cultural moral universals defend what they term 'pluralism' (the belief in incommensurable universal values) against both relativists and those who believe in an uncontentious ranking of universal values (Berlin 1991: 10–14, 78–90; Kekes 1993: 13–14, 31–5, 48–52, 118–32; Perry 1998: 64–5; Spegele 1996: 212–27).

5. *Identity*$_{ii}$: A fifth possibility also concerns identity. It applies where HRs and an ET (or ETs) enjoin the same conduct and the reasoning underlying it expresses the same core idea, but this reasoning is spelt out in different ways by the HRs and ET. To see this, we should employ the distinction invoked by Rawls between a 'concept' and a 'conception' (Rawls 1972: 4–5), where the former refers to a basic idea and the latter refers to ways of explicating that abstract idea. Drawing on this, we arrive at the following possibility: HRs and an ET can be described as identical$_{ii}$ when they prescribe the same actions and their reasons are the same (at the concept level) even if the way they are developed (at the conception level) varies.[6]

An example may be helpful here. Consider, for example, someone who defends human rights on the Kantian grounds that persons are inviolable ends-in-themselves and who eschews religious arguments. Consider also a religious believer who is utterly unaware of Kantian moral theory and who thinks that persons are sacred and that God's creation should not be tampered with. Both affirm the status of humans, but explicate this in quite different ways (Perry 1998).

Further light can be shed on identity$_{ii}$ if we consider recent debates in the philosophy of religion and comparative religion. There are two approaches that illustrate what I mean by identity$_{ii}$, namely, those that have been termed 'pluralism' and 'inclusivism'. Common to both positions is the belief that the world's major religions share the same spiritual and moral beliefs when expressed in a highly abstract way, but that these religions interpret these core tenets in different ways. Pluralists argue that each of these different interpretations is equally valid and none is privileged. A leading exponent of the pluralist view is John Hick (1989: 231–96; 1995: especially 11–30). Deploying Kant's distinction between *noumenon* and *phenomenon*, he argues there is an ultimate reality (a *noumenon*), but that people perceive it in different ways (the *phenomena*). In this way, people may share the same conclusions, giving the same reasons (at a concept level), but elaborate those reasons in varying fashions.[7]

Inclusivism, like pluralism, maintains that the dominant world religions express at an abstract level the same basic core values and ideals, but, unlike pluralism, it denies that they are all equally valid interpretations of the same ultimate reality. From an inclusivist perspective, one perspective represents the best construal of ethical and spiritual truth. One clear and cogent statement of this approach is provided by Gavin D'Costa (1986: Ch.4).

We do not have to arbitrate between these two perspectives here. What is salient in this context is their shared belief that underlying religious differences there are common values and ideals.

6. *Apparent incompatibility:* HRs and ETs are apparently incompatible when they prescribe dissimilar actions for different people, but when the disparities arise because the people face different situations. Thus, (6) refers to situations in which people in society X and people in society Y affirm dissimilar courses of action, but the dissimilarities do not express different moral convictions but common moral convictions applied in different socio-economic-political environments (Brink 1989: 200; P. Jones 1994: 214–15). This logical possibility has long been recognised. St Augustine in his *Confessions* wrote, for example, that by 'this law [God's law] the moral customs of different regions and periods were adapted to their places and times, while that law itself remains unaltered everywhere and always' (St Augustine 1998: 44). Much more recently, Thomas Scanlon invokes what he terms 'parametric universalism', where this maintains that 'actions that are right in one place can be wrong in another place, where people have different expectations, or where different conditions obtain' (Scanlon 1998: 329).

Some, it should be noted, have invoked this logical possibility in an unconvincing and unacceptable fashion. Some east-Asian leaders (such as Lee Kwan Yew and Mahhathir Mohammed) have maintained that civil and political human rights should not be pursued in their countries because they are inimical to the economic development which is needed to escape poverty. The logical implication of this argument is that where poverty has been overcome, human rights can be appropriately pursued. This particular argument is, however, neither a convincing deployment of (6) nor a credible argument against civil and political rights. As Amartya Sen has persuasively argued, it fails because there is no convincing mechanism explaining why denying these rights furthers economic growth. Indeed, we have good reason to think that freedom of expression and democratic government furthers economic development because they enable people to articulate their economic needs. Furthermore, the empirical examples cited in defence of this argument (the success of economies such as South Korea and Singapore) can be better explained by other factors (Sen 1999: 91–3).[8]

7. *Potential Compatibility/convergence/identity:* HRs and an ET can be said to be in this position when the ET in question is not, at present, *compatible with* or *convergent on* or *identical with* HRs, but certain elements of the tradition might be developed so that they are.

As analysts of traditions frequently emphasise, traditions are rarely, if ever, static (An-Na'im 1987; MacIntyre 1988; 1990). A natural consequence of the dynamic and malleable character of ethical traditions is that traditions which oppose some human rights may adapt or evolve in such a way that they no longer conflict with those rights. This possibility has been explored by An-Na'im in his analysis of contemporary Islam. As he writes:

> The genesis of the same norms, I believe, can be found in almost all major cultural traditions. It may take some innovative reinterpretation of traditional [Islamic] norms to bring them into complete accord with the present formulation of the international standards, but the essence of these standards is already present. (An-Na'im 1987: 3–4, see also 14, 17.)

In this way, ethical traditions which are currently antagonistic toward certain human rights may be revised in ways that lessen this conflict. Such evolution is possible because within any tradition there are always different elements, different strands of thought. This enables members of traditions creatively to interpret their tradition, gradually repudiating or downplaying aspects of it that have previously been central and emphasising other aspects that have previously been marginal.

This concludes the taxonomy of possible logical relationships between human rights and ethical traditions. There may, of course, be other possibilities and the taxonomy is certainly not intended to be exhaustive. It does, however, provide a more nuanced taxonomy than the dualistic one that often operates.

Before concluding this section, two further points should be made. The first is a terminological point. In the remainder of this paper, I shall refer to all cases where HRs and ETs do not conflict (that is, cases (2) to (7)) simply as cases where HRs and an ET are in 'harmony'. Thus 'harmony' subsumes compatibility, convergence, identity$_i$, identity$_{ii}$ and potential compatibility/convergence/identity.

Second, this article has spoken thus far and will continue to speak of whether traditions as a whole are or are not in harmony with human rights. This, however, is a considerable simplification. Ethical traditions always affirm a number of principles and values. Consequently, it may be the case that whilst some aspects of an ethical tradition do conflict with human rights, others do not. Consider, for example, Islam. As I mentioned above, many maintain that in its treatment of apostasy and women, Islam conflicts with the liberal values affirmed by most contemporary western traditions. It is worth recording then that in other respects there is far less disagreement. Muslims, for example, affirm a duty to aid the suffering and overcome poverty. In addition, Islamic just-war theory corresponds to those prevalent in the west. As Bassam Tibi writes:

> When it comes to the conduct of war, one finds only small differences between Islam and other monotheistic religions or the international laws of war. ...As in other traditions, two categories of restrictions can be distinguished: restrictions on weapons and methods of war, and restrictions on permissible targets. And, just as other traditions sometimes permit these constraints to be set aside in extreme situations, in Islamic law (*shari'a*) we find the precept 'Necessity overrides the forbidden' (*al-darura tubih al-mahzurat*). (Tibi 1996: 133.)

Generalisations about whether Islam is or is not compatible with human rights are, therefore, too crude and one gets a far more accurate picture of the extent to which Muslims and human rights theorists can agree by disaggregating traditions and considering which aspects are in conflict and which are in harmony or mutual support. For brevity's sake, I shall continue to refer simply to ETs, but it should be recognised in all instances that this is simply a shorthand and traditions comprise many disparate elements, some of which may be in harmony with rights whilst others may be antithetical.

The Moral Significance of the Relationship Between Rights and Other Ethical Traditions

Thus far I have examined the nature of the possible relationships between human rights and other ethical traditions. I now want, in this section, to explore why this relationship is morally significant. To what extent does it matter if human rights are in harmony with many aspects of many non-western traditions of thought? In addition, do adherents to human rights and to ethical traditions have any reason to explore the relationship between the two?

I argue in this section that they do. I outline four reasons as to why we should examine the relationship between HRs and ETs, three of which argue that harmony between them is desirable, before then examining a challenge to the ideal of harmony between HRs and ETs. The first reason for analysing the relationship between HRs and ETs concerns moral theory and the justifiability of people's moral principles. As fallible creatures individuals have no assurance that they have indubitable knowledge of correct moral principles. Given this, when someone encounters opposing views he cannot simply dismiss them out of hand: to do so would be to assume rather than to justify his own belief's validity. It follows from this, then, that if someone is to be able to justify his beliefs, he must consider the contrary case and either be able to defeat the challenge or revise his current beliefs to meet the challenge. It also follows that a person's moral principles are more plausible and have greater legitimacy if they can overcome criticism from competing ethical traditions.[9] Human rights theorists should thus take seriously the communitarian challenges issued by contemporary Confucians and examine whether their claims are persuasive. A blind refusal to consider competing approaches is thus a form of philosophical arrogance and reflects undue confidence in one's current beliefs. Such unthinking and complacent parochialism leaves one epistemically handicapped.

There are two ways in which someone might resist this claim. They might, first, argue that ethical traditions are incommensurable and that proponents of one moral tradition (such as one affirming human rights) are unable to comprehend other radically different moral traditions (such as, for example, the moral schemes of non-western, non-individualistic cultures). The translation necessary to evaluate the challenges raised by competing traditions is thus not possible. The case for considering the alternatives expressed by different systems of thought is thereby undermined. The central premise of this counter-argument is, however, unconvincing. As Donald Davidson and Hilary Putnam have both persuasively argued, one can identify something as a tradition or conceptual scheme only if one can comprehend it and thereby grasp that it is a tradition or conceptual scheme (as opposed to something else). Recognising untranslatable conceptual schemes is thus incoherent. In addition, attempts to defend this kind of incommensurability tend to be self-undermining. To make good the claim, the protagonist of incommensurability must draw attention to a radically different conceptual scheme, but in being able to describe and relate that scheme, they undercut their own thesis by showing that what is allegedly alien and untranslatable is, in fact, translatable (Davidson 1973–74: 6; Putnam 1981: 114–15).

Given the failure of this challenge, a critic might respond by arguing that different ethical traditions encounter a different type of incommensurability. Rather than claiming that adherents to one tradition (say, one affirming human rights) cannot comprehend the central claims of some other traditions, it might be argued that the ideals adhered to by members of other traditions are so different that they can have no appeal to us.[10] Considering the views expressed by other traditions, this argument maintains, is pointless because their value-systems are so alien to ours that they do not speak to our situation. This dismissal of the claims of other traditions is, however, simply unwarranted. It is premature because we can only reach the conclusion that we can learn nothing from another tradition or traditions in an a posteriori fashion, after engaging in a process of understanding and evaluation. We cannot assert this conclusion without considering the evidence. Furthermore, even a brief consideration of traditions other than our own reveals that we often benefit from a consideration of other less familiar perspectives. To take one example, those obsessed with construing all social life in terms of individual rights and entitlements can, I suggest, benefit from the Confucian emphasis on the case for 'arbitration' as opposed to an exclusive focus on 'adjudication' of pre-set principles (Wong 1992: 776–7). Confucianism's emphasis on negotiation and harmony represents, I think, an important alternative to the litigious approach adopted by those fixated on rights.

Neither of the two invocations of incommensurability, thus, undermines the first claim advanced, namely, that our moral judgements are more defensible if they are informed by an understanding of moral traditions other than our own and are able to incorporate their insights or explain why they should be rejected. Those who are committed to human rights must therefore explore the relationship between human rights and other ethical traditions. In addition, they must show *either* that other moral ideals are in harmony with human rights *or* that they are not, but that they are less important than human rights.

A second reason for exploring the nature of the relationship between human rights and other ethical traditions is that it is important that political principles secure people's consent. Without this, those principles lack *legitimacy*.[11] The central idea being expressed here is that human rights regimes enjoy authority and legitimacy to a greater extent if people consent to them or, at least, do not reject them. Exploring the relationship between human rights and ETs is thus important if human rights regimes are to enjoy legitimacy and if they are to overcome the charge that they are alien impositions. Now, this rationale for exploring the possibility of harmony is one that is affirmed by the western contract tradition, but it also quite clearly animates some non-western leaders and intellectuals who vehemently object to the imposition of values that, it is claimed, are not their own.

Now, there are two ways in which exploring whether HRs and ETs are in harmony fosters legitimacy. First, and most straightforwardly, international norms affirming human rights gain in legitimacy if we find harmony between them and non-western ethical doctrines. Second, such international norms also gain in legitimacy if westerners engage in the same process, examining their own doctrines in the light of human rights norms and exploring the compatibility or otherwise between the two.[12] Western states who enjoin African, Latin American and Asian states to respect human rights are frequently criticised on the grounds that they are in no place to lecture other societies given their current and historical records. Given this, it is important that western states do not exempt themselves from any scrutiny that they require others to undergo. The legitimacy of international human rights law is thus doubly strengthened if members of both western and non-western moral traditions explore the relationship between those doctrines and human rights and seek to examine the possibility of harmony between HRs and ETs.

A third distinct, but related, reason for examining whether HRs and ETs are in harmony concerns order. The point here is simply that human rights norms and international law, if they are to be effective, must be stable. This, in turn, is greatly facilitated if those norms (at the very least) do not conflict with moral traditions or converge on them or even are identical with them. Long-standing stability and order cannot be secured through brute force and coercion. It requires, rather, that global norms (such as human rights) and local cultures peacefully coexist.[13]

A fourth and final reason for examining the relationship between human rights and other ethical doctrines is a pragmatic one. Many of those who resist human rights (both in the west and in non-western countries) profess themselves to be cultural relativists. They, accordingly, object to human rights on the grounds that these are a western invention and hence should be applied only in the west. Such claims are often made by conservatives and realists in the west as well as by leaders of non-western countries. There are various responses to such claims, but one important strategy is to call into question their factual assumption that the values affirmed by human rights are, in fact, repudiated by members of non-western societies. To do this requires further examination of the relationship between human rights and the values which, so it is asserted, conflict with those rights.

Lest these four points be misunderstood, several clarificatory points should be made. The first is that the first reason issues in a different conclusion to the second, third and fourth reasons. The first, recall, shows that those committed to human rights should show *either* that human rights are in harmony with ETs *or* that they are not, but that they are a less worthy ideal. It does not necessarily call for harmony between HRs, on the one hand, and all ETs, on the other. The second, third and fourth reasons, by contrast, do argue that those who are committed to HRs have good reason to value harmony between HRs and ETs. In short, whereas the second, third and fourth considerations would find it a matter of regret if there is no harmony, the first would not in cases in which adherents to HRs have considered ETs and given reasons why ETs that conflict with HRs may be sacrificed. Unlike the first consideration, then, the second, third and fourth reasons are particularly interested in whether a certain conclusion obtains (namely, are HRs in harmony with ETs?).

A second point: the second, third and fourth reasons provide reasons for valuing harmony between HRs and ETs, but it does not follow that this value is the only or the weightiest reason for action. Indeed, one can quite reasonably maintain that one should act on one's own best judgement of the case. If, therefore, after an examination of the reasons one is acting on and the countervailing reasons posed by other people's moral traditions, one comes to the conclusion that the countervailing reasons are unpersuasive then, I believe, one may act on that belief. Put another way, it would be implausible to claim that one may never act on a principle if others dissent from it. This is a recipe for inaction and the perpetuation of the *status quo*. Harmony is thus of value, but it is not of overriding value.

Many would dispute this concern for harmony between HRs and ETs and I now want to consider one often-voiced challenge to this project. It objects that a concern for finding consensus among all or most ethical doctrines, on the one hand, and human rights, on the other, results in homogeneity and submerges difference.[14]

This objection is, however, quite implausible. Harmony between HRs and ETs requires only some agreement between HRs and ETs. It is thus mistaken to assume that it stipulates an identity of views – it maintains only that adherents to ETs accept some basic rules and that within those rules they may do whatever they wish. In addition, it fails to understand the obvious point that the whole rationale for human rights is that they protect people and enable them to pursue their diverse and different conceptions of the good (Booth 1999: 55; C. Jones 1999: 175). Without those rules, people's room for variety is radically diminished and for some is destroyed altogether.

A Case Study: Theravada Buddhism

Thus far this paper has examined the *nature* of the relationship between human rights and ethical traditions, and the *moral significance* of that relationship. I now want to move from a theoretical discussion of the possible logical relations between HRs and ETs to apply it to one specific ethical tradition. As I stated in the introduction, one of the standard assumptions in discussions of human rights is that they are in conflict with non-western ethical traditions. My aim in this section is to consider to what extent this is true. It is, of course, not possible to survey all non-western ethical traditions and I shall thus focus on one example, that of Theravada Buddhism.

This tradition is worth concentrating on for several reasons. First, it is one of the world's major religions, enjoying support in Sri Lanka, Burma, Nepal, Tibet, Thailand, Laos and Cambodia. Moreover, Buddhist values are explicitly invoked by democracy movements in both Burma and Tibet. Aung San Suu Kyi (1991; 1997) has published various works invoking Buddhism to ground her democratic vision. In addition, the Dalai Lama (1999) maintains that Buddhism is committed to human rights. Given the prominence of these views and the degree of support this tradition enjoys, it is of both theoretical and practical significance if there is harmony between HRs and this ET.

A second reason for examining Theravada Buddhism is that, while there has recently been considerable academic interest in the relationship between east-Asian values and human rights, there has been little on Buddhism's position *vis-à-vis* human rights. Daniel Bell's helpful survey of east-Asian values and their attitude to human rights discusses, for example, Confucianism and Islam, but not Buddhism (Bell 1996: 641–67). Similarly, Yash Ghai (1996) provides a thorough analysis of east-Asian values, but does not discuss Buddhism. Others have explored the congruence or lack of congruence between Chinese values and human rights (Tao 1990). There have also been discussions of Hinduism (Donnelly 1989: 125–42).

Furthermore, a large amount has been written on whether Confucianism can accommodate or support human rights (Ames 1988; de Bary 1988; 1998; Chan 1999; Rosemont 1988). Lastly, there has been a great deal of attention on whether Islam is compatible with human rights, for example, by Abdullahi An-Na'im (1987; 1999) and Mayer (1994). There has, by contrast, been very little sustained analysis of Buddhism's position on human rights. There have been some exceptions. Charles Taylor illustrates his ideal of a global overlapping consensus with a discussion of Buddhism (Taylor 1999: 133–7). In addition, Buddhist scholars such as Damien Keown have addressed the question of Buddhism's relationship with rights (Keown 1995; 1996: 109–12).[15] This notwithstanding, Buddhism, in general, and Theravada Buddhism, in particular, have not been the subject of much analysis by those working on human rights. For this reason, it is worth analysing this area.

A final reason for focusing on Theravada Buddhism is that it provides a good counter-example to the dogma that non-western traditions are illiberal and incompatible with liberal egalitarian ideals of justice and rights.[16] To make good this claim, this section will begin with a brief outline of Buddhism's central tenets; show that its moral doctrines *converge* with human rights; and argue, further, that they can indeed generate a Buddhist argument for human rights.

Central Tenets

Let us begin then with an account of Theravada Buddhism. To do this, it is best to give a characterisation of Buddhism first. Stated baldly, Buddhism's main teachings are encapsulated in four central tenets, namely, the 'four noble Truths'.[17] These state, first, that there is *dukkha*, where the latter refers to both suffering and to a lack of anything permanent. Everything is transitory and belief in anything lasting (such as a self) is, therefore, a delusion. This illusion has many harmful consequences, leading people to strive for what is unattainable. The second truth is that there is a cause of *dukkha* and the third states that there is a cure for this. The fourth and final truth outlines the way to overcome *dukkha* and provides an eightfold path of action which should produce fulfilment and escape from *dukkha*. These are, of course, very bald statements and the rest of Buddhist doctrine supplements them with an account of metaphysics and ethics. The Theravada school of Buddhism that I shall concentrate on is a more traditional brand of Buddhism, staying closer to the original texts than other schools (for example, the Mahayana school). It is predominantly practised in south-east Asia.[18]

Convergence on Human Rights

Now, drawing on this, we may consider Theravada Buddhism's relationship to human rights. What is clear here is that Buddhist teachings are, at the very least, compatible with human rights and often converge on human rights. To see this, consider three considerations. First, Buddhism's moral code enjoins people to observe five precepts: not to kill, steal, commit adultery, lie and drink alcohol (Harvey 1990: 199; Keown 1996: 104; Rahula 1990: 80). These do not generate rights in others,[19] but they do prescribe and condemn the same actions as a system in which people have the right to property and not to be killed. They result thus in the third relationship outlined in the first section of this article: convergence. This convergence is further supplemented by Buddhism's emphasis on toleration: 'Who is tolerant to the intolerant, peaceful to the violent, free from greed with the greedy – him I call a Brahmin.' (Mascaro 1973: 91.)

Consider, second, Buddhism's account of the ten duties of a ruler. These enjoin a ruler to: (1) be generous, (2) adhere to the five precepts, (3) serve his subjects' interests, (4) be honest, (5) be kind, (6) not lead a profligate lifestyle, (7) not act out of hatred or hold grievances, (8) be non-violent and foster peace, (9) be tolerant and understanding, and

(10) act in accordance with the wishes of his subjects (Rahula 1990: 84–6).[20] Whilst not implying rights, these duties do require the same conduct as a system of liberal rights. They preclude cruel and intolerant policies (in duties (5), (8), and (10)). They enjoin a concern for the people's well-being (in duties (1), (3), (5), (7), (8), and (9)). In addition, the tenth rule converges on the democratic principles favoured by western thinkers (Aung San Suu Kyi 1991: 172–3). The ten duties, thus, also result in convergence with HRs, prescribing the same conduct, but for very different reasons.

Lastly, Buddhist texts enjoin rulers to meet the economic needs of their subjects. This is brought out most clearly in one of the Long Discourses: the *Cakkavatti-Sihanada Suttanta*. The latter includes a parable on the malign consequences that ensue if a king does not provide welfare to overcome poverty. Such a decision, it says, leads to poverty and this leads to an increase in theft. When this, in turn, is met by a tough law-and-order policy by the king, thieves are inclined then to turn violent to protect themselves and to lie if caught (Rhys Davids and Rhys Davids 1977b: 65–8). The account then gets more far-fetched (Rhys Davids and Rhys Davids 1977b: 68–70). What is important here is that this Buddhist text calls for political authorities to distribute resources to the needy and, furthermore, that it does so by drawing on a credible line of reasoning (poverty causes crime). It thus derives a conclusion (namely, that rulers should alleviate the needs of the poor) that converges on the welfare-state policies endorsed by egalitarian liberals.[21] A polity formed on Buddhist lines thus would be one which is tolerant, meets people's basic needs and enjoins concern and respect for others.

A Buddhist Argument for Human Rights

We can, indeed, go further than this and I want to suggest that Buddhist reasoning provides a plausible case for human rights. Given their account of well-being, Buddhists, I argue, have good reason to embrace human rights. As Keown writes in his analysis of Buddhist approaches to human rights, 'the most promising approach will be one which locates human rights and dignity within a comprehensive account of human goodness, and which sees basic rights and freedoms as integrally related to human flourishing and self-realization' (Keown 1995: 16).[22] This conclusion can be supported by two crucial features of well-being.

First, Buddhists maintain that, given the sources of misery and lack of fulfilment, the only person who can bring about fulfilment for someone is that person himself or herself. This is made clear in the following passage from the *Dhammapada*: 'By oneself the evil is done, and it is oneself who suffers: by oneself the evil is not done, and by one's Self one becomes pure. The pure and the impure come from oneself: no man can purify another.' (Mascaro 1973: 59.) Again: 'It is you who must make the effort. The Great of the past only show the way. Those who think and follow the path become free from the bondage of MARA [evil].' (Mascaro 1973: 75.) The implication of both of these passages, then, is that other people are unable to enable you to live a fulfilling life. This conclusion, moreover, is not a peripheral or dispensable feature of the Buddhist account of well-being. It is, rather, the logical upshot of the Buddhist account of *dukkha* and its causes. For Buddhists, a person's lack of fulfilment and well-being arises from him or her being dominated by 'cravings' and illusions (Mascaro 1973: 85). These flaws can only be overcome by the individual suffering them. Buddhist texts therefore enjoin: 'Live as islands unto yourselves, brethren, as refuges unto yourselves, take none other as your refuge, live with the Norm as your island, with the Norm as your refuge, take none other as your refuge.' (Rhys Davids and Rhys Davids 1977b: 74.)

The path to nirvana, then, can be attained only by an individual for himself or herself through self-control (Mascaro 1973: 69, 75, 88).[23] It follows from this that force by others is inapplicable: humans can flourish only if left free to make their own decisions and to exercise control over their life.[24] We may conclude that the Buddhist account of well-being implies that people have an interest in conducting their own life on the basis of their decisions. If we conjoin this with the most plausible account of rights, namely, the 'interest' theory of rights (Raz 1986: Ch.7), we reach the conclusion that, given this interest, people have rights to conduct their life on the basis of their judgements. A concern for well-being thus justifies rights to freedom of belief, expression and conduct.

A second feature of the Buddhist account of well-being, which is also supportive of human rights, is the Buddhist emphasis on 'liberation'. One of the central features of well-being, for Buddhists, is that it is an ideal of emancipation, a state in which persons are not dominated by their desires or 'cravings'. For Buddhists, this enslavement to any specific end or desire is a source of unhappiness and persons should seek not to be controlled by their ends, but to be free from them. Buddhism, thus, enjoins 'a life of freedom' (Mascaro

1973: 47) and calls for people to be 'free from passion and hate and illusion – with right vision and a mind free, craving for nothing both now and hereafter' (Mascaro 1973: 37). Its central injunction, then, is that persons should not be addicted to specific ends or desires and should liberate themselves from such cravings. The latter enchain people and, accordingly, lead to unhappiness.

Now, there is a striking similarity here with contemporary liberal ideals of autonomy, which similarly emphasise that persons should not be bound by any specific end and which emphasise the value of the capacity to revise and reject their conception of the good. The importance of revisability has been brought out, famously, by Allen Buchanan (1975) and such themes are commonly emphasised by Kymlicka (1989: 13) and Rawls (1993: 19, 30, 302, 312–5).[25] Now, as western liberals appeal to this conception of autonomy to support rights, so Buddhists can invoke the same interest (in not being defined by any one end and being able to revise any end) to support rights. The reasoning would proceed as follows: people can flourish only if they are autonomous and are not tied down to any specific end. Human rights protect autonomy: they provide individuals with the space to revise and adapt their ends and not be in thrall to one specific end. Therefore, a Buddhist ideal of liberation provides support for liberal rights.

Now clearly, more discussion of these two links between well-being and rights is needed. What even this brief analysis suggests, however, is that the Buddhist account of well-being provides a credible case for human rights. It is, of course, distinct from western justifications in many ways. In the first place, it provides an interesting contrast with the Rawlsian approaches to rights prevalent in the west in that it does not provide a 'political' justification of rights (which draws on the values of the public culture), but is one grounded in a 'comprehensive doctrine' (Rawls 1993). In addition, the account of well-being on which it is predicated differs from those advocated by most western perfectionists. It is, moreover, grounded in a metaphysics (that there is no underlying self) that most western liberals reject (Rawls 1972: 28–30), although it should be noted that one distinguished western liberal, Derek Parfit, explicitly defends the Buddhist conception of personal identity (Parfit 1986: 273, 280, 502–3).[26] The above Buddhist arguments thus represent a cogent non-western teleological or perfectionist vindication of human rights. Theravada Buddhism, thus, provides an interesting counter-example to the assumption that non-western traditions are inegalitarian and intolerant, producing an ethic which is tolerant and respectful of others and which supports a state that meets people's economic needs and provides people with the liberty to flourish.

Conclusion

It is time to conclude. In this paper, I have sought to explore the ways in which HRs may relate to ETs and to counter the dualistic assumption that ETs either affirm rights or reject them. Second, I have argued that we should explore the relationship that actually obtains between rights and the doctrines people espouse. Doing so enriches our understanding of both, and there are three weighty reasons as to why a reconciliation between rights and ETs is desirable. Lastly, I moved from the theoretical to the applied and in examining one case study have sought to argue that one major non-western world-view is compatible with and even supportive of human rights. Simplistic assertions that human rights are in conflict with non-western cultures are, therefore, too sweeping, and they unhelpfully obscure points of agreement. What is needed is more analysis of how rights actually relate to ethical traditions rather than a priori assertions that rights cohere only with the values of western societies.

NOTES

1. More generally, see Zolo (1997: 60–61, 63–4).
2. See also Taylor (1998: 37–8, 48–53).
3. See, for example, Berlin (1982: xxxi–xxxii, lii–liii), Bok (1993: 352–4, 356–8), Graham (1996: 143–6), Harbour (1995: 155–6, 162–6), Hart (1997: 193–200), Kekes (1993: 18–19, 31, 33, 38–42, 49, 118–32), Kung (1997: 94–9, 110–11), Matilal (1989: 357–9), Moore (1972: 1–2), Renteln (1990: Ch.4), Brandt (1959: 285–8), Perry (1998: 63–71), and Walzer (1987: 23–4). See, further, Parekh (1999: 135, 141–50). See too Pogge, who proposes a 'value-based world order' (1989: 227) based on some common ground (1989: 227–36).
4. Many draw on human nature to ground a list of common goods. Stuart Hampshire, for example, writes that some 'moral injunctions and prohibitions are explained and justified, when challenged, by reference to the unvarying dispositions and needs of normal human beings, living anywhere in any normal society: for example, the requirement not to cause suffering when this can be avoided' (Hampshire 1983: 143). See, further, Hampshire (1983: 128, 142, 143). See also Nussbaum (1992) and, in particular, her list of ten universal human goods (Nussbaum 1992: 222).
5. This constitutes a partial reply to those who maintain that there is no convergence on any substantive non-trivial moral norms: C. Brown (1999: 108) and P. Jones (2000: 35). For two competing views on the philosophical significance of convergence, see

Michael Smith (1994: 187–9) and Bernard Williams (1985: 132–55 (especially 136, 151–2), 171–2).

6. See, further, Walzer (1994: 1–19) for an extended use of the notion of thin universal concepts combined with culturally enriched conceptions. For an analysis of the limitations of this move, see P. Jones (1994: 216–17).

7. Needless to say, this use of the term 'pluralism' should not be confused with that employed by Berlin, Kekes, Perry and Spegele, which I discussed in my analysis of (4).

8. For a comprehensive critique of the argument that rights must be sacrificed for economic development, see Goodin (1979: 31–42). See, further, Donnelly (1989: 164–83) on the weakness of arguments for sacrificing economic justice for economic growth and (Donnelly 1989: 184–202) on the weakness of arguments for sacrificing political justice for economic growth.

9. My account, here, is indebted to two very different thinkers, namely, J.S. Mill and Alasdair MacIntyre. See Mill (1982: 75–118). For MacIntyre's illuminating account of moral enquiry and the revision of moral beliefs, see MacIntyre (1988: especially 354–6; 1990: especially 180–81). In particular, he provides an instructive account of 'epistemological crises' and what constitutes a successful resolution of them (MacIntyre 1988: 362). Unlike MacIntyre, however, I think that Davidson's critique of incommensurability is persuasive and also that the liberal tradition survives his critique. For another important discussion of the justification of traditions, see Taylor (1993: 215–26).

10. See, for example, David Wong's distinction between incommensurability of 'translation', 'justification' and 'evaluation' (Wong 1989: 140–58, esp. 140). The first type of commensurability I identified corresponds to his incommensurability of 'translation', whereas the second corresponds to his incommensurability of 'justification' and 'evaluation'. See also Williams (1985: 161–7) on the relativism of distance.

11. This value is uppermost in Abdullahi An-Na'im's defence of a cross-cultural approach to human rights. See An-Na'im (1987: 3; 1992a: 3, 5; 1992b: 20–21; 1999: 153). See also Parekh (1999: 139–40).

12. This important point is made by An-Na'im (1999: 153–4).

13. Some invoke similar considerations to my second and third reasons, but do not distinguish between legitimacy and stability. An-Na'im, for example, appears concerned with both legitimacy and stability, but does not differentiate between them (compare references in note 10). See also Perry, who rightly points out that 'internal critiques' are often more persuasive than an approach which invokes standards a people find alien and remote (Perry 1998: 76–7).

14. For one example of this line of reasoning, see Kenneth Surin's critique of John Hick (Surin 1990: 77–89).

15. See also Inada (1982; 1990), Thurman (1988) and Unno (1988). For Buddhism's treatment of women, see Satha-Anand (1999: 193–211).

16. As I have said, Buddhism has largely been ignored by human rights theorists. What is more, one of the very few to have mentioned Buddhism at all, Antonio Cassesse, has written that: 'In the Buddhist conception, society is patterned on the family: the political leader – the emperor, in the past – is like the father of a family, with all the powers, authority and responsibilities of the *pater familias*. Freedom therefore consists not in guaranteeing a space free from possible invasion or oppression by the authorities, but in harmonizing as far as possible the individual's action with the leader's, in view of the duty of obedience owed to the latter.' (Cassesse 1994: 53.) Cassesse does not provide any argument or textual support for this claim and, in what follows, I argue that it misconstrues Theravada Buddhism.

17. For a clear summary of the four noble truths, see the T.W. Rhys Davids and C.A.F.

Rhys Davids translation of the *Maha Satipatthana Suttanta* (1977a: 337–45).

18. My understanding of Buddhism is indebted to several excellent accounts: Gombrich (1988), Harvey (1990), Keown (1996) and Rahula (1990). For a superb account of Buddhism's political thought, see Collins (1998: Ch.6).

19. For a contrary view, see Keown (1996: 100–111). For further discussion, see Keown (1995: 9–10, 18–19). For criticism see Ihara (1998) who also denies that human rights are compatible with Buddhism.

20. See, further, Collins (1998: 460–61) and Aung San Suu Kyi (1991: 170–73).

21. Another relevant text is the *Kutadanta Sutta*, a discourse in which a ruler is advised to play an active role in the economy, subsidising farmers, supplying capital to traders and giving salaries and food to civil servants (Rhys Davids 1977: 176). For further analysis of the *Cakkavatti-Sihanada Sutta*, see Collins (1998: 480–96) and Gombrich (1988: 83–4). For analysis of the *Kutadanta Sutta*, see Collins (1998: 479–80) and Gombrich (1988: 82–3).

22. See, further, Keown (1995: 16–18, 20). As Keown writes elsewhere, 'In Buddhism, it seems that human dignity flows from the capacity of human beings to gain enlightenment.' (Keown 1996: 111.) He adds that 'By virtue of this common potential for enlightenment, all individuals are worthy of respect, and justice therefore demands that the rights of each individual must be protected.' (Keown 1996: 112.) Keown does not, however, fill out the link between the Buddhist account of well-being and human rights in the way I have suggested.

23. In his account of how Buddhism coheres with human rights, Charles Taylor also briefly notes that for Buddhism 'each individual must take responsibility for his or her own Enlightenment' (Taylor 1999: 134). He tends, however, to pursue a second distinct line of reasoning, drawing attention to 'a new application of the doctrine of nonviolence, which is now seen to call for a respect for the autonomy of each person' (Taylor 1999: 134). He thus emphasises what he terms 'the *ahimsa* [non-violence] basis for rights' (Taylor 1999: 137).

24. For a similar line of reasoning in defence of liberal rights, see Dworkin (1990) and Kymlicka (1989: 12–13).

25. For instructive discussions of autonomy, see Christman (1989) and G. Dworkin (1989).

26. One might go further and suggest that Buddhist writings provide support for a social contract view of legitimate power. In particular, one of the Long Discourses (*Digha Nikaya*), called the *Agganna Sutta*, discusses the creation of the earth and human society and at one point suggests that power arises through consent (Collins 1993: 345–6) equating the ruler with he who is 'Appointed by the people' (Collins 1993: 345). Commentators on this text have persuasively argued that it is not a positive argument for the social contract, but more a critique of the idea that some are born to rule over others (Collins 1998: 448–51; 1993: 387–9; Gombrich 1988: 85–6).

REFERENCES

Ames, R., 1988. Rites as rights: The Confucian alternative. In *Human Rights and the World's Religions*, ed. Rouner, L. Notre Dame (IN), University of Notre Dame Press.

An-Na'im, A. 1987. Religious minorities under Islamic law and the limits of cultural relativism. *Human Rights Quarterly*, Vol.9.
1992a. Introduction. In *Human Rights in Cross-Cultural Perspectives: A Quest for Consensus*, ed. An-Na'im, A. Philadelphia, University of Pennsylvania Press.
1992b. Toward a cross-cultural approach to defining international standards of human rights: The meaning of cruel, inhuman, or degrading treatment or punishment.

In *Human Rights in Cross-Cultural Perspectives: A Quest for Consensus*, ed. An-Na'im, A. Philadelphia, University of Pennsylvania Press.

1999. The cultural mediation of human rights: The Al-Arqam case in Malaysia. In *The East Asian Challenge for Human Rights*, eds. Bauer, J. and Bell, D. Cambridge, Cambridge University Press.

Aristotle. 1986, *The Politics*, trans. Sinclair, T.A., revised and represented Saunders, T. Middlesex: Penguin.

Augustine, St. 1998, *Confessions*, trans. Chadwick, H. Oxford: Oxford University Press.

Aung San Suu Kyi. 1991, *Freedom from Fear and Other Writings*, ed. and introduction Aris, M. London: Penguin.

1995. Freedom, development, and human worth. *Journal of Democracy*, Vol.6, No.2.

1997, *The Voice of Hope: Conversations with Alan Clements with Contributions by U Kyi Maung and U Tin U*. London: Penguin.

de Bary, W., 1988. Neo-Confucianism and human rights. In *Human Rights and the World's Religions*, ed. Rouner, L. Notre Dame (IN), University of Notre Dame Press.

1998, *Asian Values and Human Rights: A Confucian Communitarian Perspective*. Cambridge (MA): Harvard University Press.

Bell, D., 1995. Democracy in Confucian societies: The challenge of justification. In *Towards Illiberal Democracy in Pacific Asia*, Bell, D., Brown, D., Jayasuriya, K. and Martin Jones, D. New York, St. Martins Press.

1996. The east Asian challenge to human rights: Reflections on an east-west dialogue. *Human Rights Quarterly*, Vol.18.

1997. A communitarian critique of authoritarianism: The case of Singapore. *Political Theory*, Vol.25, No.1.

Berlin, I., 1982. Introduction. In *Four Essays on Liberty*. Oxford, Oxford University Press.

1991, *The Crooked Timber of Humanity: Chapters in the History of Ideas*, ed. Hardy, H. London: Fontana.

Bok, S. 1993. What basis for morality? A minimalist approach. *The Monist*, Vol.3.

Booth, K., 1999. Three tyrannies. In *Human Rights in Global Politics*, eds. Dunne, T. and Wheeler, N. Cambridge, Cambridge University Press.

Brandt, R. 1959, *Ethical Theory: The Problem of Normative and Critical Ethics*. Englewood Cliffs (NJ): Prentice-Hall.

Brink, D. 1989, *Moral Realism and the Foundations of Ethics*. Cambridge: Cambridge University Press.

Brown, C., 1999. Universal human rights: A critique. In *Human Rights in Global Politics*, eds. Dunne, T. and Wheeler, N. Cambridge, Cambridge University Press.

Buchanan, A. 1975. Revisability and rational choice. *Canadian Journal of Philosophy*, Vol.5, No.3.

Cassesse, A. 1994, *Human Rights in a Changing World*. Cambridge: Polity.

Chan, J., 1999. A Confucian perspective on human rights for contemporary China. In *The East Asian Challenge for Human Rights*, eds. Bauer, J. and Bell, D. Cambridge, Cambridge University Press.

Christman, J. (ed.) 1989, *The Inner Citadel: Essays on Individual Autonomy*. Oxford: Oxford University Press.

Collins, S. 1993. The discourse on what is primary (*Agganna Sutta*). An annotated translation. *Journal of Indian Philosophy*, Vol.21, No.4.

1998, *Nirvana and other Buddhist Felicities: Utopias of the Pali imaginaire*. Cambridge: Cambridge University Press.

Dalai Lama. 1999. Buddhism, Asian values, and democracy. *Journal of Democracy*, Vol.10, No.1.

D'Costa, G. 1986, *Theology and Religious Pluralism: The Challenge of Other Religions*. Oxford: Blackwell.

Davidson, D. 1973–74. On the very idea of a conceptual scheme. *Proceedings and Addresses of the American Philosophical Association*, Vol.47.

Donnelly, J. 1989, *Universal Human Rights in Theory and Practice*. Ithaca and London: Cornell University Press.

Dower, N. 1998, *World Ethics: The New Agenda*. Edinburgh: Edinburgh University Press.

Dworkin, G. 1989, *The Theory and Practice of Autonomy*. Cambridge: Cambridge University Press.

Dworkin, R., 1990. Foundations of liberal equality. In *The Tanner Lectures on Human Values: Volume XI*, ed. Peterson, G. Salt Lake City, University of Utah Press.

Ghai, Y., 1996. Human rights and governance: The Asia debate. In *Human Rights Law*, ed. Alston, P. Aldershot, Dartmouth.

Gombrich, R. 1988, *Theravada Buddhism: A Social History from Ancient Benares to Modern Colombo*. London and New York: Routledge.

Goodin, R. 1979. The development-rights trade-off: Some unwarranted economic and political assumptions. *Universal Human Rights*, Vol.1, No.2.

Graham, K., 1996. Coping with the many-coloured dome: Pluralism and practical reason. In *Philosophy and Pluralism*, ed. Archard, D. Cambridge, Cambridge University Press.

Gyeke, K. 1997, *Tradition and Modernity: Philosophical Reflections on the African Experience*. New York: Oxford University Press.

Hampshire, S. 1983, *Morality and Conflict*. Oxford: Blackwell.

Harbour, F. 1995. Basic moral values: A shared core. *Ethics and International Affairs*, Vol.9.

Hart, H.L.A. 1997, *The Concept of Law*, second edition, postscript eds. Bulloch, P. and Raz, J. Oxford: Clarendon Press.

Harvey, P. 1990, *An Introduction to Buddhism: Teachings, History and Practices*. Cambridge: Cambridge University Press.

Hick, J. 1989, *An Interpretation of Religion: Human Responses to the Transcendent*. London: Macmillan.

1995, *The Rainbow of Faiths: Critical Dialogues on Religious Pluralism*. London: SCM.

Horigan, D. 1996. Of compassion and capital punishment: A Buddhist perspective on the death penalty. *The American Journal of Jurisprudence*, Vol.41.

Ihara, C. 1998. Why there are no rights in Buddhism: A reply to Damien Keown, In *Buddhism and Human Rights*, ed. Keown, D., Prebish, C. and Husted, W. Surrey: Curzon.

Inada, K., 1982. The Buddhist perspective on human rights. In *Human Rights in Religious Traditions*, ed. Swidler, A. New York, The Pilgrim Press.

1990. A Buddhist response to the nature of human rights. In *Asian Perspectives on Human Rights*, eds. Welch, C. and Leary, V. Boulder, Westview.

Jones, C. 1999, *Global Justice: Defending Cosmopolitanism*. Oxford: Oxford University Press.

Jones, P. 1994, *Rights*. London: Macmillan.

2000. Human rights and diverse cultures: Continuity or discontinuity? *Critical Review of International Social and Political Philosophy*, Vol.3, No.1, special issue.

Kekes, J. 1993, *The Morality of Pluralism*. Princeton: Princeton University Press.

Keown, D. 1995. Are there 'human rights' in Buddhism? *Journal of Buddhist Ethics*, Vol.2.

1996, *Buddhism: A Very Short Introduction*. Oxford: Oxford University Press.

Kung, H. 1997, *A Global Ethic for Global Politics and Economics*. London: SCM.

Kymlicka, W. 1989, *Liberalism, Community, and Culture*. Oxford: Clarendon Press.

MacIntyre, A. 1988, *Whose Justice? Which Rationality?* London: Duckworth.

1990, *Three Rival Versions of Moral Enquiry: Encyclopaedia, Genealogy, and Tradition*. London: Duckworth.

Mascaro, J. 1973, *The Dhammapada: The Path of Perfection*, introduction and trans. Mascaro, J. London: Penguin.

Matilal, B.K., 1989. Ethical relativism and confrontation of cultures. In *Relativism: Interpretation and Confrontation*, ed. and introduction Krausz, M. Notre Dame (IN), University of Notre Dame Press.

Mayer, A.E. 1994. Universal versus Islamic human rights: A clash of cultures or a clash with a construct? *Michigan Journal of International Law*, Vol.15.

Mill, J.S. 1982, *On Liberty*, ed. and introduction by Himmelfarb, G. Middlesex: Penguin.

Moore, B. 1972, *Reflections on the Causes of Human Misery and upon Certain Proposals to Eliminate Them*. London: Penguin.

Nussbaum, M. 1992. Human functioning and social justice: In defence of Aristotelian essentialism. *Political Theory*, Vol.20.

Parekh, B., 1999. Non-ethnocentric universalism. In *Human Rights in Global Politics*, eds. Dunne, T. and Wheeler, N. Cambridge, Cambridge University Press.

Parfit, D. 1986, *Reasons and Persons*. Oxford: Oxford University Press.

Perry, M.J. 1998, *The Idea of Human Rights: Four Inquiries*. New York: Oxford University Press.

Pogge, T. 1989, *Realizing Rawls*. Ithaca and London: Cornell University Press.

Putnam, H. 1981, *Reason, Truth, and History*. Cambridge: Cambridge University Press.

Rahula, W. 1990, *What the Buddha Taught*. London: Wisdom.

Rawls, J. 1972, *A Theory of Justice*. Oxford: Oxford University Press.
  1993, *Political Liberalism*. New York: Columbia University Press.

Raz, J. 1986, *The Morality of Freedom*. Oxford: Clarendon Press.

Renteln, A. 1990, *International Human Rights: Universalism versus Relativism*. London: Sage.

Rhys Davids, T. W., 1977. *Kutadanta Sutta*. In *Dialogues of the Buddha: Part I*, trans. Rhys Davids, T. W. from the Pali of the Digha Nikaya. London, Pali Texts Society.

Rhys Davids, T. W. and Rhys Davids, C.A.F., 1977a. *Maha Satipatthana Suttanta*. In *Dialogues of the Buddha: Part II*, trans. Rhys Davids, T. W. and Rhys Davids, C.A.F. from the Pali of the Digha Nikaya. London, Pali Texts Society.
  1977b. *Cakkavatti-Sihanada Suttanta*. In *Dialogues of the Buddha: Part III*, trans. Rhys Davids, T. W. and Rhys Davids, C.A.F. from the Pali of the Digha Nikaya. London, Pali Texts Society.

Rosemont Jr., H., 1988. Why take rights seriously? A Confucian critique. In *Human Rights and the World's Religions*, ed. Rouner, L. Notre Dame (IN), University of Notre Dame Press.

Satha-Anand, S., 1999. Looking to Buddhism to turn back prostitution in Thailand. In *The East Asian Challenge for Human Rights*, eds. Bauer, J. and Bell, D. Cambridge, Cambridge University Press.

Scanlon, T. 1998, *What We Owe to Each Other*. Cambridge (MA): Harvard University Press.

Sen, A. 1997. Human rights and Asian values. Sixteenth Morgenthau Memorial Lecture on Ethics and Foreign Policy. New York, Carnegie Council on Ethics and International Affairs.
  1999. Human rights and economic achievements. In *The East Asian Challenge for Human Rights*, eds. Bauer, J. and Bell, D. Cambridge, Cambridge University Press.

Smith, M. 1994, *The Moral Problem*. Oxford: Blackwell.

Spegele, R. 1996, *Political Realism in International Theory*. Cambridge: Cambridge University Press.

Surin, K. 1990. A certain 'politics of speech': 'Religious pluralism' in the age of the McDonald's hamburger. *Modern Theology*, Vol.7, No.1.

Tao, J. 1990. The Chinese moral ethos and the concept of individual rights. *Journal of Applied Philosophy*, Vol.7, No.2.

Tatsuo, I., 1999. Liberal democracy and Asian orientalism. In *The East Asian Challenge for Human Rights*, eds. Bauer, J. and Bell, D. Cambridge, Cambridge University Press.

Taylor, C., 1993. Explanation and practical reason. In *The Quality of Life*, eds. Nussbaum, M. and Sen, A. Oxford, Clarendon Press.

1998. Modes of secularism. In *Secularism and its Critics*, ed. Bhargava, R. Delhi, Oxford University Press.

1999. Conditions of an unforced consensus on human rights. In *The East Asian Challenge for Human Rights*, eds. Bauer, J. and Bell, D. Cambridge, Cambridge University Press.

Thurman, R., 1988. Social and cultural rights in Buddhism. In *Human Rights and the World's Religions*, ed. Rouner, L. Notre Dame (IN), University of Notre Dame Press.

Tibi, B., 1996. War and peace in Islam. In *The Ethics of War and Peace: Religious and Secular Perspectives*, ed. Nardin, T. Princeton, Princeton University Press.

Unno, T., 1988. Personal rights and contemporary Buddhism. In *Human Rights and the World's Religions*, ed. Rouner, L. Notre Dame (IN), University of Notre Dame Press.

Walzer, M. 1987, *Interpretation and Social Criticism*. Cambridge (MA): Harvard University Press.

1994, *Thick and Thin: Moral Argument at Home and Abroad*. Notre Dame (IN): University of Notre Dame Press.

Williams, B. 1985, *Ethics and the Limits of Philosophy*. London: Fontana.

Wong, D., 1989. Three kinds of incommensurability. In *Relativism: Interpretation and Confrontation*, ed. and introduction Krausz, M. Notre Dame (IN), University of Notre Dame Press.

1992. Coping with moral conflict and ambiguity. *Ethics*, Vol.102, No.4.

Zolo, D. 1997, *Cosmopolis: Prospects for World Government*, trans. McKie, D. Cambridge: Polity.

5

The Pendulum Theory of Individual, Communal and Minority Rights

TOM HADDEN

Some political theorists and some lawyers have a rather simplistic view of the nature of human rights. One part of the problem is the idea that human rights can be deduced from, or at any rate linked to, the nature of the human individual. Another is the idea that human rights are in some sense absolute and unchanging and can therefore be used as a basis for the development of global theories of democracy and governance. A third is the idea that all human rights are of equal status and that none can be subordinated to any other. All of these ideas are seriously misleading and must be corrected before there can be any useful interchange between human rights lawyers and political theorists.

These are broad claims which cannot be fully explored in this contribution to the debate on global citizenship. All that can be attempted in this context is a brief explanation of a more balanced and realistic approach to the nature of human rights and their relevance to political and social theory. It may help to begin by identifying more precisely the nature of the misunderstandings which have caused the problems. For ease of reference, they have been called the individualistic fallacy, the absolutist fallacy and the equal-status fallacy, though as might be expected the underlying issues are matters of degree and emphasis, rather than rights and wrongs. Then, by way of more practical illustration, an account will be given of the development of human rights principles in respect of minorities. This will demonstrate the way in which accepted human rights principles in this area have swung to and fro like a pendulum. It may also help to show the relevance to critical social and political theorists of the flexibility of human rights.

The Individualist Fallacy

The essence of the individualistic fallacy is that human rights are founded on, or can be deduced from, the nature of human beings as individuals and can therefore only be granted to, or recognised for, individual human persons. This view was clearly expressed in the American Declaration of Independence[1] and the French Declaration of the Rights of Man and the Citizen,[2] which laid the foundation for modern human rights thinking. It has been incorporated in Article 1 of the Universal Declaration of Human Rights[3] and, as will be seen, in some of the more recent formulations of minority rights. But it is somewhat misleading. Though most of the currently accepted range of human rights are best expressed as belonging to individuals, others make sense only in the context of larger groups of individuals and a few are explicitly granted to larger groups as such.

The rights which are most obviously individual are those such as the right to life (ECHR: Art.2; ICCPR: Art.6),[4] the right not to be tortured (ECHR: Art.3; ICCPR: Art.7) or the right to a fair trial (ECHR: Art.6; ICCPR: Art.14), which are intended to protect individuals as such from state abuses. So too are those such as the rights to free expression (ECHR: Art.10; ICCPR: Art.19) and privacy (ECHR: Art.8; ICCPR: Art.17), which are designed to guarantee the freedom of individuals from certain forms of interference. But others, such as the rights to free association (ECHR: Art.11; ICCPR: Art.22) and to freedom of religion (ECHR: Art.9; ICCPR: Art.18), can in practice be enjoyed only in the context of group activities and might as well be thought of as the rights of groups as of their individual members. In respect of larger communities or groups, generally referred to as minorities, there is continuing dispute among human rights lawyers, as will be seen, as to whether the rights recognised in the relevant human rights instruments are properly to be regarded as group rights or merely as the rights of their individual members. Few rights, of which the right of self-determination (ICCPR: Art.1; ICESCR: Art.1)[5] is the prime example, are granted exclusively to collective groups or peoples.

It may reasonably be claimed therefore that, while it is logically possible to formulate almost all accepted human rights as the rights of individuals either in their own right or as members of groups or minorities, it is more sensible to accept that there is a continuum of rights, some of which are granted exclusively to individuals, some of which are, in effect, granted both to groups and to their individual members, and some of which are granted exclusively to groups as such.

It may be added that this is a very satisfactory reflection of the nature of human society as it is analysed by social scientists. Most sociologists and political scientists would certainly be surprised to be told that families and associations and communities and ethnic groups did not have as significant a place in human society as the individuals of which they are composed.

The Absolutist Fallacy

The idea that all human rights are absolute and unchanging is equally misleading. Very few of the established range of rights are absolute in any real sense of the word. The prohibition of torture and inhuman and degrading treatment (ECHR: Art.3; ICCPR: Art.7) is the prime example. Almost all are qualified by specific or general limitation clauses or provisos. The right to life, which is often portrayed as the most fundamental of all human rights, is subject to very significant exceptions under the European Convention on Human Rights, covering capital punishment and the use of force where it is absolutely necessary in defence against unlawful violence, for lawful arrest and prevention of escape, and to quell riots and insurrections (ECHR: Art.2).[6] Most other civil and political rights are subject to broad limitation clauses. For example, the right to freedom of assembly and association under the European Convention is subject to such restrictions 'as are prescribed by law and are necessary in a democratic society in the interests of national security or public safety, for the prevention of disorder or crime, for the protection of health or morals or for the protection of the rights and freedoms of others' (ECHR: Art.11) and the right of peaceful assembly under the International Covenant on Civil and Political Rights to such restrictions as are 'imposed in conformity with the law and which are necessary in a democratic society in the interests of national security or public safety, public order (*ordre public*), the protection of public health or morals or the protection of the rights and freedoms of others' (ICCPR: Art.21). There are significant variations in the limitation formula used in respect of other relevant rights, but all include the phrase 'necessary in a democratic society' without further explanation of what that may involve. Most can also be suspended by a formal act of derogation in time of war or other public emergency threatening the life of the nation (ECHR: Art.15; ICCPR: Art.4).[7]

This means, in effect, that adjudications on alleged violations of human rights by international bodies such as the European Court of

Human Rights and the United Nations Human Rights Committee involve a large degree of discretion in balancing a wide range of competing considerations. As might be expected, this has resulted in a good deal of variation in the principles of interpretation and the standards applied under the main human rights conventions. In particular, all the international bodies have granted what is called a 'wide margin of appreciation' to individual states in the implementation of their human rights obligations, especially in respect of matters of public and private morality and during states of emergency.[8]

In addition, international human rights standards themselves are subject to periodic change and development as new international conventions and declarations are adopted. This process is not usually based on any sustained theoretical analysis of the nature of human rights.[9] It is more often a reflection of the prevailing consensus within the various international bodies concerned, which in practical terms is the essential precondition for the recognition of international human rights. The result is that there are from time to time quite substantial shifts in the focus of attention and in the priorities granted to certain types of human rights. This is especially noticeable in respect of matters of major political or economic significance, such as rights relating to population control, or the resolution of international or internal conflicts, or measures to promote economic equality and, in particular, as will be seen, the rights of minorities and indigenous peoples.

The Equal Status Fallacy

The idea that all human rights are of equal status is closely related to the idea that they are in some sense absolute. It has been given formal support in a number of declarations by the international human rights community, notably the section of the Vienna Declaration of 1993 which proclaimed the 'universality, indivisibility and interdependence' of all human rights and called on the international community to 'treat human rights globally in a fair and equal manner, on the same footing and with the same emphasis'.[10] But these declarations have been adopted mainly as a means of resolving the continuing dispute between states in the west, which have tended to give primacy to traditional civil and political rights, and those in the Third World, which have tended to give primacy to economic and social rights. In practice, there is a clearly established hierarchy of human rights, not least in the sense that some are given stronger protection than others in the procedures for implementation and adjudication.

At the top of the hierarchy are those few rights, notably the prohibitions on torture (ECHR: Art.3; ICCPR: Art.7) and slavery (ECHR: Art.4; ICCPR: Art.8), which are not subject to limitations of any kind and from which no derogation is permitted under any circumstances. These are followed by other non-derogable rights,[11] such as the right to life (ECHR: Art.2; ICCPR: Art.6) and the prohibition of retrospective criminalisation (ECHR: Art.7; ICCPR: Art.15), which are subject to certain limitations. Next come the main body of civil and political rights, which are subject both to general limitations and to derogation during states of emergency, but in respect of which states can be held responsible for violations by the various international adjudicatory bodies. At a somewhat similar level are the main body of economic and social rights in respect of which states are not required to give immediate effect, as opposed to using their best efforts to achieve compliance over time.[12] Lastly, there is a huge range of international human rights declarations and principles which are not formally binding and in respect of which there is no procedure for adjudication.[13]

The implications of this hierarchy for the theory and practice of globalisation are similar to those in respect of individualism and absolutism, that human rights are not fixed but flexible, and that the degree of importance accorded to each set of rights can and does alter over time and in response to changing ideological and political priorities. All these points can be forcefully illustrated in respect of the development of the theory and practice of minority and communal rights.

The Development of Minority and Communal Rights: The Pendulum Effect

One of the most striking features of international human rights law and political practice in respect of minorities is its variability. Over the years there has been a continual and, at times, a cyclical progression in the formulation and application of minority rights in response to changing ideologies and changing political priorities. In this sense, it is arguable that minority rights, more than most other human rights, have been subject to what may be called a pendulum effect: that from time to time the focus of attention has shifted from individual to group rights and back again rather like a pendulum. This may be demonstrated by a brief account of the development of human rights law and political practice in this area.

In the eighteenth century, there was an almost exclusive emphasis in the American Declaration of Independence and the French Declaration of the Rights of Man and the Citizen on the rights of the individual as opposed to the group or community. This may perhaps be related to the prevailing political and economic theories in which individuals were thought to be independent actors who made their own political, social and economic contracts.[14]

During the nineteenth century, there appears to have been a general shift toward the recognition of peoples and classes as primary political and social entities to which individuals belonged, whether they liked it or not. The new science of sociology focused attention on such concepts as *volkgeist*, group psychology and class interests.[15] This was reflected primarily in the ideals of the nation-state and class politics. But it also led to an increased interest in the identification and accommodation of minorities. The first modern minority-protection treaties were negotiated in the Balkans toward the end of the nineteenth century (Giordan 1992).

The problem of how to deal with minorities which could not be fitted neatly into the newly constructed patchwork of nation-states then became one of the primary political concerns after the war of 1914–18. In some cases, the preferred solution was the mass transfer of people into suitably homogeneous states, as in the case of Greeks and Turks.[16] The more common response was the negotiation of bilateral minority treaties which had the backing of the League of Nations and were to be enforced as an integral part of international law (Thornberry 1992: Ch.3). The distinction between individual and group rights does not appear to have been recognised as creating any major theoretical or practical difficulties during this period. But the fact that the treaties were often ignored and that the existence of ethnic minorities was used as an excuse for German aggression soon brought the concept of minority recognition into some disrepute.

After the war of 1939–45, attention shifted back again to the exclusive protection of individual human rights. The emerging consensus on international human rights law, as expressed in the Universal Declaration of Human Rights (UDHR) in 1948 and the European Convention on Human Rights and Fundamental Freedoms in 1950, focused almost exclusively on the protection of individuals from unjustified state interference and from any form of discrimination based on group identity (UDHR: Art.2; ECHR: Art.14). The assimilation of immigrants into a tolerant liberal society was the order of the age. The only surviving reference to the rights of groups was the

TABLE 1
THE RELATIONSHIP BETWEEN POLITICAL THEORY AND HUMAN RIGHTS
FORMULATIONS

Period	Ideological Basis	Human Rights
Late eighteenth to mid-nineteenth century	Focus on individual under the influence of individualistic theories of political economy	American Bill of Rights and French Declaration of Rights of Man
Mid-nineteenth to early twentieth century	Focus on national and class rights under the influence of sociology and socialism	Minority rights treaties and League of Nations
Mid-twentieth century	Focus on individual rights in reaction to World War II and on the prevention of discrimination	Universal Declaration and European Convention on Human Rights
Late twentieth century	Resurgence of interest in minority and indigenous rights	UN Declaration and European Framework Convention on the Protection of National Minorities

reference to self-determination in Article 1(2) of the United Nations Charter, which probably had more to do with the pressure for decolonisation than with the acceptance of the validity of group rights. It was not unusual in this period for human rights experts to deny that a human right could properly be vested in anyone but an individual (Sieghart 1986: Ch.18). Those involved in formulating Article 27 of the International Covenant of Civil and Political Rights of 1966, which was the first reassertion of the rights of minorities after a lengthy period of silence, could not bring themselves to express minority rights in other than individual terms.[17]

More recently the pendulum has swung back again toward the recognition of group and minority rights, notably in the International Labour Organisation's Convention 169 on Indigenous and Tribal Peoples of 1989, the Copenhagen Document of the Organisation for Security and Co-operation in Europe of 1990, the United Nations Declaration on the Rights of Persons Belonging to National or Ethnic, Religious or Linguistic Minorities of 1994, and the European Framework Convention on the Protection of National Minorities of 1994. This has much to do with the increasing recognition of, and guilt about, the destruction by western societies and values of traditional and indigenous societies and cultures. It may also be related to the re-emergence of ethnic and religious groups as a powerful social and political force in many countries. It was certainly well underway before the collapse of the Soviet empire forced the issue of minority rights back into the forefront of the international political and human rights agenda. But events in former Yugoslavia and elsewhere are already causing some reaction and a reassessment of the need to protect the rights of individuals against enforced and unwanted communal separation and conflict. The most recent human rights instruments on minorities have included provisions guaranteeing the rights of individuals not to be treated as members of ethnic or religious groups against their will.[18] These developments and the relationship between prevailing political theory and human rights formulations are summarised in Table 1.

The Continuum of Individual and Group Rights

This approach can be further developed by identifying a range or continuum on which claims to individual and collective rights may be placed. At the individual end of the continuum, as illustrated in Table 2, the emphasis is on the right of individual members of a group not to be discriminated against on the basis of their communal, religious or ethnic identity, a right clearly recognised in the European Convention on Human Rights and many other international conventions (ECHR: Art.14; ICCPR: Art.2). The only political right which is granted at this point on the continuum is the individual right to vote (ECHR: Protocol 1, Art.3; ICCPR: Art.25). Close to this position is the recognition of the right of members of minority groups to practise their religion, use their language and express their culture in community with others, notably under Article 27 of the International Covenant on Civil and Political Rights. Somewhat further along the continuum is the recognition of a right of members of minority communities to equality in employment, to state funding for separate schools and to a measure of political control over their own local affairs. Rights of this kind are now granted in a number of countries under national legislation[19] and have been given some international recognition in the recently adopted United Nations Declaration on the Rights of Persons Belonging to National or Ethnic, Religious or Linguistic Minorities of 1992[20] and the European Framework Convention for the Protection of National Minorities of 1994.[21] In countries or regions where there are two or more major communities, such as South Tyrol and Northern Ireland, there may be further recognition under national legislation of the right of members of each community to a proportional share in public or private employment and to a proportional share in regional or national government,[22] though this level of communal recognition and accommodation has not, as yet, been accepted in international human rights instruments. The most extreme position on the continuum is the recognition of the right of peoples to self-determination, notably under the common Article 1 of the International Covenants on Civil and Political Rights and Economic, Social and Cultural Rights, though there is, of course, little international consensus on the criteria by which a people entitled to a right to self-determination is to be distinguished from a minority which is not granted that right (Musgrave 1997).

TABLE 2
A CONTINUUM OF INDIVIDUAL AND GROUP RIGHTS

Basis of claim	Nature of claim	Human rights recognition
Individual members of group	Right not to be discriminated against	ECHR art. 15 ICCPR art. 26 CERD/CEDAW
	Right to vote	ICCPR art. 25 ECHR Prot. 1
Members of minority	Right to practise religion, language and culture with others	ICCPR art. 27
Communities and indigenous peoples	Right to communal equality in employment;	National statutes
	right to establish separate schools;	EFCPNM art. 13
	right to effective participation in governing own affairs	EFCPNM art. 15
Divided societies	Quotas in employment; power-sharing in national government	National statutes
Nations/territorial populations	Self-determination; self-government;	ICCPR/ICESCR ART. 1
	territorial integrity/self-defence	UN Charter arts. 2(4) and 51

[UDHR = Universal Declaration on Human Rights; ECHR = European Convention on Human Rights; ICCPR = International Covenant on Civil and Political Rights; ICESCR = International Covenant on Economic, Social and Cultural Rights; CERD = Convention on the Elimination of All Forms of Racial Discrimination; CEDAW = Convention on the Elimination of All Forms of Discrimination Against Women; EFCPNM = European Framework Convention on the Protection of National Minorities]

It is clear that the numerical size of a communal or ethnic group is of crucial significance in determining an appropriate level of recognition on this continuum. The larger the communal group, the greater are the rights which are typically claimed or granted. In this sense, numbers matter and the argument that all human rights are essentially individual becomes less and less convincing. But this is an issue on which human rights conventions are, as yet, undeveloped, though the principle that minorities of different kinds, in terms of numbers and physical distribution within a state, may be entitled to different levels of recognition has already been raised in the relevant United Nations bodies.[23]

Parallel Rights?

Whether there is a direct correlation in the swing of the pendulum in respect of the various areas in which rights are claimed or granted is less clear. If there were, it should be possible to devise a field or matrix through which the pendulum might swing, as illustrated in Figure 1.

FIGURE 1
THE HUMAN RIGHTS PENDULUM

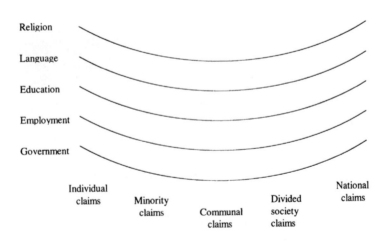

The implications of this formulation for the development of human rights principles and theories of globalisation clearly require some further consideration. If a correlation of this kind were to be established as a norm, it would be possible to prescribe more precisely the types of right which could legitimately be claimed by communal and ethnic groups of different sizes. But it is not clear that this is, or should be, a universal objective. There is an important political choice to be made in dealing with distinctive communal and ethnic groups between policies of recognition within integrative structures for government, education and employment and policies of recognition by the provision of separate governmental and educational institutions. This choice may well have significant longer term implications for the stability of the states and societies concerned. It is certainly not at all clear that the same policy objectives should be prescribed in all circumstances or that human rights lawyers, rather than politicians and political scientists, are the best people to make the choice. In this, as in some other fields, there is a danger that human rights lawyers may be seeking to impose their principles and norms in matters on which they have no real expertise or understanding. There is also a danger that those interested in theories of global citizenship and governance may too readily accept that normative human rights principles can provide a firm basis for their work.

Conclusions

The point of this brief summary of 200 years of legal and political development is not to suggest that those involved did not recognise or understand the issues. No experienced social scientist or historian expects to find many ideas or arguments that are completely new. It is to emphasise that there is a genuine difference between political and legal structures in which the principal focus is on individuals as opposed to communities or on individual as opposed to group rights, and, second, that there is a real choice to be made between them. It does not follow that there is a single correct answer to be found, any more than there is a correct position for a pendulum. But it is certainly as important for social and political scientists and for politicians and human rights lawyers to understand the nature of the cyclical processes in which they are involved as for natural scientists to understand the motion of a pendulum.

A second point is that the approach in most international covenants and declarations on minority (or communal) rights is often unclear and unhelpful in many respects. There is clearly a need for clarification of the application of the right to self-determination in situations in which two or more communities are intermingled. There is also a need for more detailed provisions on the issues of communal integration and separation, and on the permissible forms of positive discrimination. Advance on all these issues may well require the development of more practical and pragmatic guidelines on appropriate or permissible measures in particular situations. In addition, it may be necessary for this purpose to distinguish more clearly between communities (or minorities) of different sizes, types and distributions in relation to the population at large.

A more general conclusion of special significance for political theorists is that the most appropriate formulations on issues of democracy and governance in complex societies are unlikely to be found in human rights conventions and declarations. It may be more helpful to recognise the essentially political choices which are involved in dealing with the balance between individual and communal rights, rather than to suggest that solutions may be found in human rights principles. As has already been suggested, on matters of this kind the human rights pendulum swings to and fro over time. Just as economists have to come to terms with the need to understand and manage the business cycle as best they can, so must human rights lawyers and political theorists come to terms with the need to understand and manage the swings of the pendulum between individual and communal rights.

NOTES

1. 'We hold these truths to be self-evident, that all men are created equal, that they are endowed by their Creator with certain inalienable Rights, that among these are Life, Liberty and the pursuit of Happiness.'
2. 'Les hommes naissent et demeurent libres et égaux en droits. ...Le but de toute association politique est la conservation des droits naturels et imprescriptibles de l'homme. Ces droits sont la liberté, la propriété, la sûreté et la résistance à l'oppression.'
3. 'All human beings are born free and equal in dignity. They are endowed with reason and conscience and should act towards one another in a spirit of brotherhood.'
4. All references to specific articles of the European Convention on Human Rights and Fundamental Freedoms (ECHR) and the International Covenant on Civil and Political Rights (ICCPR) will be given in this abbreviated form.
5. International Covenant on Economic, Social and Cultural Rights (ICESCR).
6. The corresponding provision in ICCPR (Art.6), that 'no-one shall be *arbitrarily* deprived of his life' (emphasis added), is less specific, but has been interpreted in

broadly the same way.

7. For a detailed discussion of the application of the right to derogate during states of emergency, see Oraa (1992).
8. For a critical discussion of this doctrine, see O'Donnell (1982).
9. For a detailed account of the negotiations leading to the adoption of the Universal Declaration on Human Rights in 1948, see Humphrey (1984).
10. Vienna Declaration and Programme of Action adopted at the Second World Conference on Human Rights (1993: Para.3).
11. The list of non-derogable rights is not identical in the main international covenants, but the practical effect is similar (Oraa 1992: Ch.4).
12. Under Article 2(1) of the International Covenant on Economic, Social and Cultural Rights the obligation of each state party is 'to take steps, individually and through international assistance and co-operation, especially economic and technical, to the maximum of its available resources, with a view to achieving progressively the full realisation of the rights recognised in the present Covenant by all appropriate means, including particularly the adoption of legislative measures'.
13. See, for example, the United Nations Code of Conduct for Law Enforcement Officials adopted by the General Assembly in 1979, the United Nations Declaration on the Elimination of All Forms of Intolerance and Discrimination based on Religion or Belief adopted by the General Assembly in 1981, and the United Nations Declaration on the Rights of Persons belonging to National or Ethnic, Religious or Linguistic Minorities adopted by the General Assembly in 1994; documents of this kind are regularly relied on by human rights pressure groups but have no binding force; an updated list of those agreed within the United Nations entitled *Human Rights: A Compilation of International Instruments* is published from time to time by the Office of the United Nations High Commissioner for Human Rights (United Nations 1993).
14. See the works of Rousseau (*Du Contrat Social*) and Locke (*Two Treatises on Government*) in the field of political philosophy and Adam Smith (*The Wealth of Nations*) in economic theory.
15. On national influences on economics and sociology, see the works of List (*The National System of Political Economy*) in Germany and Durkheim (*De la division du Travail Social*) in France, and on class identity, see Marx's *Capital*.
16. The transfer was negotiated under the Convention of Lausanne of 1923 (Thornberry 1992: 51).
17. Article 27 reads: 'In those states in which ethnic, religious or linguistic minorities exist, persons belonging to such minorities shall not be denied the right, in community with the other members of their group, to enjoy their own culture, to profess and practise their own religion or to use their own language.'
18. European Framework Convention for the Protection of National Minorities (Art.3).
19. As, for example, in Canada under the Canadian Constitution and the Employment Equity Act 1995, and in Northern Ireland under the Education (Northern Ireland) Orders and the Fair Employment Acts (Northern Ireland) 1976 and 1989 respectively.
20. Under Article 3, persons belonging to minorities have the right 'to participate effectively in decisions on the national, and where appropriate, regional level concerning the minority to which they belong or the regions in which they live, in a manner not incompatible with national legislation'.
21. Under Article 13, states are required to recognise the right of members of minorities to set up and manage their own schools, though any obligation on the state to fund them is expressly ruled out; under Article 15, states are required to 'create the conditions necessary for the effective participation of persons belonging to national minorities in cultural, economic and social life and in pubic affairs, in particular those affecting them'.

22. The provisions for proportional power-sharing in South Tyrol are contained in the Autonomy State of 1972; those proposed for Northern Ireland are included in the Good Friday Agreement of 1998 and the Northern Ireland Act 1998.
23. See the report of the Special Rapporteur, A. Eide (1992: UN Doc.E/CN.4/Sub.2/ 1992/37).

REFERENCES

Eide, A., Special Rapporteur. 1992, *Possible Ways and Means of Facilitating the Peaceful and Constructive Solution of Problems Involving Minorities*. UN Doc.E/CN.4/Sub.2/ 1992/37.

Giordan, H. 1992, *Les Minorités en Europe*. Paris: Éditions Kimé.

Humphrey, J. 1984, *Human Rights and the United Nations: A Great Adventure*. Dobbs Ferry: Transnational Publishers.

Musgrave, T. 1997, *Self-Determination and National Minorities*. Oxford: Clarendon Press.

O'Donnell J. 1982. The margin of appreciation doctrine: standards in the jurisprudence of the European Court of Human Rights. *Human Rights Quarterly*, Vol.4, No.4, pp.474–507.

Oraa, J. 1992, *Human Rights in States of Emergency in International Law*. Oxford: Clarendon Press.

Sieghart, P. 1986, *The Lawful Rights of Mankind*. Oxford: Oxford University Press.

Thornberry, P. 1992, *International Law and the Rights of Minorities*. Oxford: Clarendon Press.

United Nations. 1993, *Human Rights: A Compilation of International Instruments*. Geneva: United Nations.

6

The Question of Self-Determination and its Implications for Normative International Theory

KIMBERLY HUTCHINGS

The notion of self-determination is central to normative debate in international theory. Mainstream ethical perspectives (cosmopolitan and communitarian) and alternative normative approaches (such as those of critical theory, post-modernism and feminism) are all concerned with examining and promoting this ideal, although with radically different understandings of what it implies, from the principle of state sovereignty to the international political recognition of sexual difference. In this article, I will be exploring the way in which the ideal of self-determination operates in a range of normative debates about individual and collective rights. Crucial to these debates are the issues of which 'self' is in question and what counts as self as opposed to other determination. For some normative theorists, the selves that should be self-determining in the international context are the selves of the individual human being, the nation and the state and for yet others they include the gendered human being or the participants in new social movements, in Falk's phrase 'citizen pilgrims' (Falk 1995: 211–12). Within each of these possibilities are concealed a host of further complex debates about why these particular entities are important and how their autonomy should be understood, accommodated and encouraged. Here both broad and specific policy issues become the object of normative judgement: is there a right to nationality? Do nations have a right to be states? Should international intervention be permitted to enforce global moral norms? Should cultural difference be respected? Should free movement of people

A fuller version of this argument can be found in Hutchings (1999: Ch.5). I am grateful to Sage Publications for permission to reprint some of the material from that chapter here.

across state borders be permitted? The list is ongoing and seemingly inexhaustible.

In the first section, some of the ramifications of the idea of the human individual as the locus of self-determination in mainstream cosmopolitan and communitarian ethical theories will be considered. It will be argued that there is a tendency toward theoretical deadlock within this kind of normative international theory. However, it will also be argued that the nature of this theoretical deadlock has less to do with the substantive conclusions reached by the various normative approaches than with their grounding in what Steiner refers to as a 'first best' world characterised by an idealised fixed ontology and the associated claim of epistemological privilege for the theorist's insight into what self-determination means (Steiner 1992: 90; O'Neill 1992: 115–9). In the second section, three alternative approaches to normative thinking about international politics will be discussed: critical theory, post-modernism and feminism. It will be argued that these critical theories go a considerable way to moving beyond theoretical deadlock, by challenging the idealised ontology through which concepts of individuals, nations and states are thought in more mainstream approaches. In the third section, some of the implications of the claims of critical theories for the project of making normative judgements in the international context will be teased out. In conclusion, I will suggest that although critical theory, post-modernism and feminism do not break entirely with the logic of more traditional moral theorising, by abandoning reliance on an idealised moral ontology, they do point the way toward a more limited, but also more fruitful, conception of the possibilities and problems inherent in normative theory in the international context.

Which Selves? What Determination?

For many cosmopolitan international theorists the defining mark of *normative* international theory is that it is based on the ethical value of individual as opposed to supra-individual or collective selves. Cosmopolitan approaches of a liberal contractarian and Kantian kind do not simply put supreme value on the human individual, but on the idea of individual self-determination or autonomy, though they do not understand it in the same way or with the same prescriptive implications. In the case of liberal contractarian approaches, the value attached to individual self-determination is based on the idea of individual natural right. Some versions of contractarianism link this notion of natural right to ideas of natural law and reason which, as with Kantianism, connect the value of human autonomy to some notion of higher moral capacities, or, for example, to a basic moral right to property. For other versions of contractarianism, natural right is a pre-moral attribute, simply the freedom to follow natural determination toward self-preservation in a state of nature. The latter version of contractarianism is different from the former and from Kantianism in that it presumes the necessity of the institutionalisation of right in a political order, even though it legitimates that order in terms of the prior contract (an actual or hypothetical voluntary relinquishment of natural right). In liberal contractarianism, the meaning of national or state right is parasitic on the prior existence of individual right. This does not necessarily imply that collective right is not taken seriously. Contractarian arguments may underlie both arguments for an international human rights regime which will secure certain individual rights and freedoms and arguments for strong state borders to protect the rights of insiders, particularly property rights, from any outside encroachment.[1]

In the case of Kantian approaches, the value to be attached to individual self-determination is expressed in the formulation of the categorical imperative, which requires that persons should always be treated as ends in themselves and never solely as means to others' ends. The status of 'end-in-him/herself' derives in Kant's theory from the self's potential as a self-legislating being. The self is only truly valuable in so far as the self is judging and acting in accordance with the determinations of a pure will, rationally or morally. Self-determination for Kant, therefore, is understood in terms of a very specific kind of determination: not simply doing what one wills, but what one should will (he is adamant, for instance, that capital punishment is justified and even required by the higher self of the individual who has transgressed the law against murder) (Kant 1991: 143–4). The implications of the imperative to respect humans as ends in themselves are prescriptively powerful, although different Kantian theorists differ over their precise nature. One clear implication, however, is that it must be impermissible to respect the rights of national or state collectives if these are using individuals purely as means to their ends. Thus, there are many Kantian-based arguments against killing or otherwise harming innocents in both war and peace. Some are more restrictive in their scope than others, confining demands for protection of human individuals against state or interstate forces to so-called 'negative' rights against the killing of innocents, torture, suppression of freedoms of thought and speech, and so on. Others are more extensive, demanding, in addition, 'positive' protection of individuals against hunger and poverty. The crucial commonality between different types of Kantian theorising, however, is that the rights of individuals are the litmus test of social and political arrangements. Nations and states are of instrumental as opposed to intrinsic value.

Kantianism and contractarianism along with utilitarianism and Marxism have formed the main theoretical resources for discussion about what should be the nature and extent of international human rights in the current international order (Beetham 1995).[2] Common to all these debates has been the assumption that international rights were essentially attached to individuals. Metatheoretical debates, about what the basis for the idea of universal human rights might be, have been accompanied by substantive discussions as to which rights count as fundamental or secondary and how, if they exist, such universal rights should be institutionalised. In so far as the idea of international human rights has been recognised as having some validity, debate has been particularly preoccupied with the issue of negative (legal, civil, and political) versus positive (material) rights, with Kantians, utilitarians and Marxists often more favourable to the latter than contractarians (Cranston 1973; Nickel 1987: 92–119; Vincent 1992; Shue 1996). Although (particularly in relation to the implementation of human rights regimes) the cosmopolitan idea of international human rights has been recognised to be in potential tension with the international context of a nation-state system, nevertheless, this system has generally been taken for granted in cosmopolitan international theory (Vincent 1992). The right to national self-determination, which is enshrined in the UN declaration of human rights, has only recently attracted much theoretical attention from western academics. However, a debate has now opened up which directs critical attention to the privileging of human individuals in the international rights discourse of cosmopolitan theory and, in particular, the ethical priority given by Kantian and contractarian discourses to the notion of individual autonomy or self-determination. This is the debate over the right to nationality and the right of nations to self-determination or statehood. This debate has been fuelled by a combination of circumstances, including the consequences of the end of the cold war and the resurgence of nationalist movements in eastern Europe and the former Soviet Union as well as the experience of strong sub-state nationalist pressures within established western states such as Canada and the UK. The obvious significance of nationalist politics in recent years in so many parts of the world has led to the questioning of the nation-state as a normatively desirable mode of political organisation and thereby put into question the nature of the 'selves' which normative international theory seeks to empower or limit within the international arena (Tamir 1993; Miller 1995; Caney et al. 1996; Gilbert 1998).

Within mainstream normative international theory, the debate engendered by a focus on the right to national self-determination is largely concerned with mapping the relative strength of principles of individual, national and state autonomy. An excellent example of this can be found in the collection of essays *National Rights, International Obligations* (Caney et al. 1996), in which a variety of theorists debate the following interrelated issues: the question of the moral legitimacy of rights to nationality; the issue of whether moral obligations are necessarily transnational, or whether special obligations can be owed to fellow nationals; and the problem of reconciling global norms with cultural diversity both within states and transnationally (Caney et al. 1996: 1). As far as the first issue is concerned, the debate hinges on the question of whether the moral right to national self-determination is held by individuals or by nations. Much discussion, therefore, is devoted to the concept of nation. What kind of real or fictional entity is a nation and would any normative implications (such as a right to autonomy) follow from its existence? Unsurprisingly, given the vast number of conflicting definitions in social scientific and historical research into nations and nationalism, normative theorists find the concept of nation and related concepts of nationality and national identity hard to pin down (George 1996; Charvet 1996; Tamir 1996; Gilbert 1996; 1998: 8–12). Some theorists argue that the concept of a nation is too radically indeterminate to have any fixed meaning. For those that accept that the concept has meaningful reference, the nation is generally assumed to be comprised of some or all of the elements of common language, territory, culture, tradition and collective self-identity in which members of the nation recognise themselves to be such. Of particular significance in definitions of the nation in normative theory is the element of national identity and the degree of its self-consciousness. Often, the normative significance of nations and nationality depends on the extent to which individuals self-consciously identify with and value the nation (Tamir 1993: 63–9).

Two types of cosmopolitan response to the question of what normative consequences, if any, are bound up with the concept of nationhood are prominent in *National Rights, International Obligations*. I refer to these alternatives as liberal statism (Charvet

1996; Steiner 1996) and liberal nationalism (MacCormick 1996; Tamir 1996). One response (liberal statism) argues for the normative irrelevance of nationality as a prior ground for right, on the grounds that, even supposing the existence of a nation is demonstrable, nothing of normative significance follows because rights to self-determination can only be held by individuals or states. Liberal statism is derived from liberal contractarianism. On this account, collective right is state right because it can only be derived from actual or hypothetical voluntary contractual grounds and not from previously shared culture, language, territory or tradition as such (Charvet 1996). According to this argument, there are no problems with seeing obligations to fellow contractors as taking priority over obligations to outsiders, since right is generated by contract itself and the individual natural rights which underlie it. There is also a clear sense that the contractarian legitimation of right is universally valid, regardless of the existence of alternative cultural norms. As noted earlier, the liberal-statist position is a paradoxical one since it simultaneously reinforces the normative significance of individual right and can be used to defend a strong distinction between rights of individuals within and without the contractually legitimised political order. This paradox is reflected in two opposing tendencies in reading off the normative implications of liberal statism on issues such as the relation to internal cultural minorities within the state and immigration. On the one hand, for liberal statists, there are no grounds for respecting either global norms or culturally entrenched values unless they are in keeping with the political culture of contract. In principle, therefore, it seems that states could be justified in imposing contractual values on non-liberal minorities within the state or on outside communities, providing it was prudent to do so (that is, did not risk the entrenchment of individual rights which grounds the state's authority in the first place). On the other hand, the demands of national and cultural minorities within existing states has drawn liberal statists back to the question of the conditions of possibility of contractual political order and led to arguments defending the right of a given group of individuals, perhaps identifying themselves as a nation, to either reconstitute their contract entirely through secession or renegotiate it with the majority community in terms of group rights (Charvet 1996: 65). As with the Hobbesian residual right of individuals to self-defence, however, for liberal statists this carries no necessary implications for the majority community's existing rights – there is no automatic duty to respect the right to secession or to institutionalise groups rights, though it might be prudent to do so. In relation to questions of transnational migration, but particularly to emigration into established states, there is a powerful liberal-statist argument for immigration policy to be determined solely in terms of the rights of insiders (Steiner 1992: 90–92). Although this does not necessarily imply a policy of closed borders, there is no legitimate ground to protest against a commitment to closure on the part of states. However, liberal-statist arguments, particularly those which are premised on the ultimate significance of property right, have returned again to the conditions of possibility of contract and, in recent years, produced arguments for the opening up of state borders, since the individual's right to property is argued to be the fundamental ground of state right and when state rights block the individual's right to property (whether of an insider or outsider), it is state right which should give way (Steiner 1992: 90–91). As Steiner puts it:

> It is the sad fate of virtually every moral and political doctrine to be called upon to deliver judgments in given circumstances which, on its own basic principles, constitute a 'second best' situation. The result of such deliverances, more often than not, is some proposal that embarrasses those principles by advancing certain types of morally valid right at the expense of other types, whereas in a 'first-best' world all these rights would be compossible. (Steiner 1992: 90.)

The arguments of liberal statism on rights to self-determination in an international context draw attention to the consequences of a theoretical position which applies first-best criteria to second-best situations. Thus, in a perfect world, the possession of no individual rights would be at the expense of anyone else's and the mechanism of voluntary contract would govern all social and political relations. However, in an imperfect world not only does liberal statism find itself having prescriptive implications which seem contrary to its fundamental principles, but it also finds itself having to think about factors, such as national identity, for which it does not have adequate first-best conceptual equipment.

According to critics, liberal statism fails to comprehend the fact that liberal individuals and liberal states are sustained by things other than natural right and rational self-interest. In Canovan's recent work on the concept of nationhood, she has pointed to the way in which the nation is the neglected but ever-present condition of the bringing together of universal principle and particularistic identity in liberal political theory and ideology (Canovan 1996a; 1996b: 78–81). Canovan herself suggests that attempting to give explicit theoretical articulation for and legitimation to the role of nation and nationality as the mediator between individual and state or as the resolution of conflicts between inclusionary and exclusionary elements of modern citizenship is pragmatically unwise because the success of nationality as a mediating factor in modern politics is premised on its vagueness and ambiguity (Canovan 1996b: 76). However, it is precisely this which is currently being attempted by the liberal alternative to liberal statism in answering the question of justifying rights to national self-determination, the alternative of liberal nationalism.

Liberal nationalists argue for the importance of national rights to self-determination on the grounds that nationality is constitutive of and therefore matters to individuals. This approach is exemplified by the work of theorists such as Tamir (1993; 1996) and MacCormick (1996), and owes much to Lockean and Kantian liberal traditions in combination with some distinctively communitarian claims. Like liberal statists, liberal nationalists accept the primacy of individual rights to self-determination as the grounds for legitimacy of any given political order (MacCormick 1996: 35–8). However, for liberal nationalists, individual rights to self-determination are inseparable, first, from ideal models of self-determination which are, as with Kant's analysis, grounded in moral principle, and, second, from the view that individuals are always embedded in specific, constitutive cultural identities, one of which is national identity (MacCormick 1996: 42; Tamir 1993: 33). Liberal nationalists, therefore, interpret Kantian respect for individual autonomy to include respect for the national identity element which is constitutive of any particular individual, which implies the right to nationhood and nationality. However, the ideal element in Kantian conceptions of individual autonomy acts as a counterweight to the notion of absolute respect for nationality and links liberal nationalism to the promotion not of nationality as such, but of liberal nations, made up of liberal individuals (Tamir 1993: 42–8). A boundary between inside and outside is drawn between national and non-national in liberal nationalism, but the difference between obligations to insiders as opposed to outsiders is somewhere in between the inclusive and exclusive versions of liberal statism, with neither individuals, nations nor states as such having absolute rights to autonomy. Of all of these three, however, it is states which emerge as having the least normative significance. Liberal nationalism links individual and national self-determination as mutually ethically valuable while downplaying the moral significance of the principle of state sovereignty. This is because at the heart of liberal nationalism is the idea of the ethical significance for the individual of cultural identity. Individuals and cultural identities are entitled to respect because of their intrinsically valuable nature. However, states are entitled to respect only in virtue of the extent to which they protect individual rights and cultural identities (MacCormick 1996: 49; Tamir 1993: 142–67). For liberal nationalists, membership of a nation is somewhere between the voluntary contracting into a particular polity and the involuntary membership of a family. There are special obligations to fellow nationals, but these operate under constraints of duties to respect the rights of individuals in general. Liberal nationalism assumes the existence of universal global norms which include the principle of respect for national cultural difference, as long as that difference does not challenge the limits of liberal nationalism's tolerance which are marked by Kantian liberal principles of respect for individuals.

On questions such as the rights of cultural minorities within states, liberal nationalism tends to support, as might be expected, the rights of self-proclaimed national minorities to self-determination. However, this does not necessarily imply that liberal nationalism is committed to the principle that all nations must be states; it may equally favour the kind of political arrangement said to be emerging in the EU, in which local national identities are protected under a trans-state framework (MacCormick 1996: 50–51; Tamir 1993: 150–53). Alternatively, it may favour the path of multiculturalism in which existing states grant differential rights to such minority groups (Kymlicka 1995). Whereas the fundamental principles of liberal statism work against the notion of any level of right between that of the individual and state authority, liberal nationalism is apparently perfectly amenable to the recognition of sub-state national group right, as an extension of traditional liberal principles of both liberty and toleration. However, as with liberal statism, there are tensions in the liberal-nationalist position when it comes to defining what respect for rights to national self-determination within an existing multi-nation state or political order might mean. Liberal nationalists, as noted above, combine the idea of respect for individual cultural identity with respect for individual autonomy understood in a Kantian sense. For liberal nationalists, the individual right to national identity is linked to the notion that this is an identity which is at some level voluntary. This does not mean that this identity has its origin in contract or that individuals ever existed outside of their national identity. It means that national identity is something to which individuals (because they are also moral beings in a Kantian sense) are capable of having a critical relation. National identity is something which individuals can redefine or revise internally or, ultimately, it is something which individuals can come to reject and walk away from. There is, therefore, a necessary tension between liberal nationalism and the kinds of national identity which block the possibility of critique or change, or exit. Thus, when theorists such as Kymlicka provide a liberal model for the recognition of group rights, they are forced to distinguish between collective rights giving rights of 'internal restriction' to a minority group (which means that that group can limit the liberties of its individual members) and collective rights of 'external protection' which protect the minority groups against majority decisions that would undermine the basis of its existence (Kymlicka 1995: 35–44). The former are problematic for liberal nationalism, because they threaten the possibility of critique or change, or exit; the latter, Kymlicka argues, are perfectly compatible with liberal values. Clearly, however, it is very difficult to sustain the distinction between 'internal restrictions' and 'external protections' if, for instance, the survival of a particular form of community is premised on the exclusion of some individuals from education or decision making or restrictive policies on emigration from a national homeland.

Liberal-nationalist prescriptions in relation to issues of migration, particularly immigration into national communities, display similar tensions. In giving considerable weight to the idea of a national right to self-determination, liberal nationalists are particularly concerned with the protection of national cultural identity. Immigration, therefore, could in principle be restricted if it threatened the survival of national identity. However, national identity is important because it is important to individuals, and individuals have a right to self-determination in accordance with, but also in critical relation to, the identities by which they are constituted. Liberal nationalists recognise, therefore, the normative power of arguments from both political and economic migrants that they too have a right to self-determination. This leads Tamir, for instance, to argue that nations should only have the right to restrict immigration if they are exporting goods to enable less fortunate groups to be self-determining elsewhere. Liberal nationalism then becomes dependent on conditions of global distributive justice as well as other fundamental liberal values (Tamir 1993: 61).

Like most attempts to combine distinct elements in a justificatory strategy, liberal nationalism is accused by its critics of collapsing back into one or other of the elements it seeks to combine. These critics come both from the liberal tradition itself and from communitarianism. Liberal contractarian and Kantian critics accuse liberal nationalism of going too far down the slippery slope of communitarian thinking and abandoning, or putting in jeopardy, the respect for individual rights on which liberal nationalism is supposed to be premised (Charvet 1996; Caney 1996). Liberal contractarians find the notion that national identity in itself carries normative consequences incompatible with the idea of individual right and the voluntary basis of political community (Charvet 1996: 57). Kantians are concerned about the problem of discriminating between acceptable and non-acceptable national identities (Caney 1996: 133–4). According to both liberal statists and Kantians, the compatibility claimed by liberal nationalists between liberalism and national identity is the product of wishful thinking, which does not take account of the gap between the ideal world of theory and the actual 'second best' world we inhabit. Alternatively, communitarians claim that the liberal nationalists' continued endorsement of the importance of choice and moral principle means that they have failed to grasp what nationality actually means and, in practice, are bound to revert back to either liberal-statist or Kantian positions. For communitarians, the question of the right to national identity can only be answered in terms of an essentially collective as opposed to individual basis for the right to national self-determination (Walzer 1981; 1992; 1994a; 1994b; Miller 1995; 1999).

The two main variants of the liberal response to the question of the right to national self-determination are opposed, but also reflected, by two variants of a communitarian response. On the one hand, organic communitarianism rests on an analogy between the Hobbesian natural rights of individuals and the natural rights of communities. On the other hand, civic republican communitarianism, following Rousseau, rests on the assertion of a link between the moral significance of the capacity for autonomy in individuals and collective democratic self-rule. In the former case, the right to national self-determination is grounded in a nation's prior natural right to survival. In the latter case, the right of national self-determination is not grounded in the prior right of a pre-existing communal entity, but in a collectively generated 'general will', in which individuals are forged into a self-legislating body of citizens through the overcoming of their particular individual interests. The former position implies that nations, in so far as they are culturally cohesive determinate communities, should be states. The latter implies rather the opposite, suggesting that democratic states are the ideal mode of political order and that in order for them to be, they also need to be underpinned by nations. For both, however, a privileging of the rights of insiders over outsiders in the nation-state is justified. Walzer makes a distinction between thick and thin moralities which ground a norm of non-intervention (Walzer 1994a). Miller makes a distinction between obligations of right to co-nationals and obligations of humanity to foreigners, with the latter clearly being weaker than the former (Miller 1995: 73–80).

The prescriptive implications of both positions in relation to rights of national minorities and immigration are similar and apparently clear cut. In both cases, the obvious way in which to accommodate group difference is secession, since the nation-state depends on solidarities which will be weakened by deep splits between different national identities within a common citizenship. In both cases also, the right to grant membership of a national community is necessary to that community's survival and can rest only within that community and there are no externally generated rights of individuals to gain entry across borders (Walzer 1981: 32). Nevertheless, as with liberal statism and liberal nationalism, when communitarianism is applied to issues such as toleration of cultural diversity or free movement of peoples in practice, its prescriptive implications are less clear cut than might have been expected. To begin with, the actual world in no way corresponds to either the organic or republican communitarian ideal – the world does not divide into self-contained cohesive communities or participatory democracies. This has rather different implications for the two types of communitarian argument. Organic communitarianism, like liberal statism, lacks conceptual equipment to deal with the actual interdependence and entanglement that characterises existing communities. It therefore lends itself to the same kind of pragmatic compromise between first- and second-best worlds in which sources of right other than organic community gain instrumental defensibility. The recognition of the inherent significance for individuals of participating in national community leads, for instance, to Walzer's argument for the rights of individuals to asylum and the thin morality which supports the norm of non-intervention (Walzer 1992; 1994a; 1994b). There are clearly prudential grounds for limiting national right in relation to other nations. There may also be prudential reasons for a nation to accept something less than full nation-statehood, perhaps where no clear territorial partition is possible (Miller 1995: 108–18). Alternatively, there may be prudential

advantages to permeable borders between nation-states and individual
rights of migration. The situation is rather different in the case of
republican communitarianism, which, like liberal nationalism, does not
value the community (individual) purely as such but in relation to a
higher potential of the community (individual). Behind the 'higher' in
both of these cases is a universal ideal of freedom as autonomy in the
Kantian sense. In an analogous (but reversed) pattern to liberal
nationalism, republican communitarians, by identifying collective self-
determination with a higher form of will, beyond prudential self-
interest, link rights to national self-determination to rights for
individuals and states. In practice, the positions of republican
communitarians and liberal nationalists merge into support for the
liberal-democratic political community and the simultaneous
endorsement of individual and collective right, something which is
achieved in the first-best world of theory by the assumption that all
political communities take on this form in conditions which enable
mutual recognition and respect without remainder. Walzer moderates
the rights of states to control membership in the light of universal
principles (Walzer 1981: 32). Miller, like Tamir, ends up endorsing the
need for global distributive justice to underpin collective rights to self-
determination (Miller 1995: 105).

The exchange within and between liberal (cosmopolitan) and
communitarian theories on the question of the right to national self-
determination is a battle between ideals as to the priority to be given
to the values of individual, national and state autonomy. The problem
which all of these ideal accounts returns to is that of accommodating
different autonomies, both horizontally (for example, how different
individual autonomies are made compatible with each other) and
vertically (for example, how individual right is made compatible with
national or state right). A further battle of ideals is also played out
between an understanding of autonomy in terms of determination by
purely natural or purely rational will. This is reflected in the tensions
between liberal statism and liberal nationalism in their understanding
of the meaning of individual autonomy, and between organic and
republican strands of communitarianism in the understanding of
collective autonomy. Whichever idea is in question, it provides a
standard against which the actual world is always found wanting. The
noise of the battle obscures the extent to which all of these perspectives
are making very similar arguments and running into similar problems.
In relation to the first subject of battle, both liberal and communitarian
theories conceptualise the subjects of self-determination as

determinately bounded, radically distinct entities. Intersubjective, international and interstate spheres are presented as empty space in which the different selves collide, horizontally and vertically, or must somehow be forced to fit in with one another. In the case of theories (liberal and communitarian) which understand self-determination in Hobbesian terms, the accommodation of different rights is achieved through pragmatic self-interest. In the case of theories (liberal and communitarian) which understand self-determination in Kantian terms, the accommodation of different rights is achieved through universal principle. In both cases, however, the second-best world of international politics fails to live up to the first-best world of theory and the fit between individual, nation and state which is achievable in principle proves unworkable in practice. Each of the theoretical approaches is, therefore, in a position to condemn the others on grounds of hypocrisy and inconsistency.

Deconstructing Selves and Self-Determination[3]

In this section, I will be examining ways in which alternative perspectives in normative international theory approach the questions posed by the cosmopolitan-communitarian debates in the ethics of international relations: is there a moral right to national self-determination? Are moral obligations necessarily transnational or are there special obligations owed to fellow nationals? How can one reconcile global norms with cultural diversity? The meaningfulness of these questions and their answerability depends for critical theorists of the international on two key things: the ontological claims made about the being of individuals, nations and states, and the epistemic status of normative claims about the meaning of self-determination. I will examine three examples of alternative perspectives in turn: critical theory (the term generally used in international relations theory to refer to approaches influenced by Frankfurt School critical theory, in particular, by the work of Habermas), post-modernism, and feminism.

The ontology of critical theory challenges the notion of both nation and state as subjects of self-determination as they appear in liberal statist and communitarian thinking, but holds strongly to a Kantian ideal of the autonomous individual human being (Hoffman 1993; Linklater 1998). For example, Linklater's ontological position is essentially a radicalisation of the liberal-nationalist argument given above. It is a radicalisation because it goes much further than liberal nationalism in envisaging a post-Westphalian international political order and a move beyond both closed national identity and the principle of state sovereignty. This move is accomplished partly on the basis of rejecting the notion of the international as the empty spaces between nations and nation-states (Linklater 1998: 34–45). For Linklater, there is such a thing as international society which both constitutes and is constituted by a variety of levels of political and economic order; there is, therefore, no clear cut inside-outside distinction where nations and states are concerned. However, Linklater's position is still identifiable with the liberal-nationalist position because at its heart is the Kantian ideal of respect for persons as ends in themselves, with the understanding that this respect must extend to the range of identities through which a person is constituted (gendered, ethnic, national, sexual and so on) (Linklater 1998: 46–76). In Linklater's theory, as with liberal nationalism, the normative key is the capacity of individuals to engage critically with their world on the basis of moral norms. Unlike liberal nationalists, however, Linklater identifies this normative key as operating within actual institutions in a logic of self-transcendence; this is particularly evident in his account of the modern state. Where Canovan sees the fudge of nationality keeping the tensions between universality and particularity in place within the state, Linklater argues that the universal principles (such as the notion of universal human rights) work over time to transcend the nation-state linkage and enable the recognition of both particular identity and universal right in a new form of international political order (Linklater 1998: 184–9; 1999). Linklater argues that in developed western states, notably Europe, this logic of transcendence is already far advanced and needs to be articulated both for the sake of further improvement in the western context and as the basis for relation with other parts of the world in which this logic does not operate in the same way (Linklater 1998: 218; 1999). Linklater's vision of the developing world of international politics is one in which there is a coexistence between more familiar pluralist and solidarist modes of international society and a new post-Westphalian order in which the fit between sovereignty, territoriality, nationality and citizenship which kept the Westphalian order in place no longer applies (Linklater 1998: 60).

In keeping with the characteristic stance of critical theory, Linklater does not assume that the world will necessarily progress in terms of the normative key of the critical capacities of individuals. However, it is his conception of this key which explains the confidence with which he identifies what counts as progress. Here his reliance on Habermasian moral epistemology is crucial. According to Habermas, moral rightness is dependent on the agreement of moral norms in open, non-distorted dialogue between those affected by the implementation of the norm in question (Habermas 1990; Linklater 1998: 87–93). Linklater's judgement of what counts as moral progress is those institutional changes which extend the inclusion of persons affected by norms in decision-making processes over those norms and minimise morally irrelevant exclusions. More than that, however, progress is those changes which maximise the possibility of non-distorted communication in the argument over norms – a situation in which the inherent critical capacities of human individuals, their ability to be swayed by the better argument, are able to flourish. 'How to develop new forms of citizenship and community which release the potential for wider universalities of discourse which is already immanent within the modern state and international society is the central praxeological question.' (Linklater 1998: 151.)

If we return to the question of the right to national self-determination posed in the ethics of international relations, we find it answered, by Linklater, in instrumental terms which are again reminiscent of, but more radical than, liberal nationalism. Critical theory supports a right to national identity on the grounds of the right to individual autonomy, because national identities are constitutive of individuals. However, even more than with liberal nationalism, critical theory is critical of exclusive versions of national identity and is committed to opening up boundaries between communities. Moreover, critical theory gives equal weight to the range of identities constitutive of any particular individual and would not necessarily give normative priority to national identity. Linklater sees himself as building upon both cosmopolitan and communitiarian insights to move beyond the idea of nations and states as the principal modes of political order:

> Far from being antithetical, communitarianism and cosmopolitanism provide complementary insights into the possibility of new forms of community and citizenship in the post-Westphalian era. They reveal that more complex associations of universality and difference can be developed by breaking the nexus between sovereignty, territoriality, nationality and citizenship and by promoting wider communities of discourse. (Linklater 1998: 60.)

As with liberal nationalism, the fundamental understanding of moral norms in critical theory is universalistic. However, where liberal nationalism appears to get caught in tensions between the universal and particular which it cannot resolve except in an ideal world, critical theory resolves the tensions by stressing the immanent critical force which will push individuals within communities to transform them in line with greater openness. The possibility of legitimating special obligations to co-nationals or respecting cultural difference is always limited by the guiding force of the moral norms (and, therefore, the limits of toleration) implicit in modernity. This is evident in relation to the prescriptive implications of critical theory on topics such as the recognition of group rights and transnational migration. In both cases, critical theory supports principles of recognition and openness, but always in the context of the extension of dialogic possibilities in the contemporary world order. This is acknowledged by Linklater in the argument that without the implicit acceptance of the logic of inclusion which is characteristic of modernity a post-Westphalian order is unlikely to develop. Relations between liberal and non-liberal political communities cannot therefore take the same form as relations between liberal communities whether within or between existing states or transnational organisations (Linklater 1999).

Critical theory links an ontology of nations and states (which identifies them as dynamically evolving through a complex and inseparable set of internal and external determinations) together with the notion of a logic of moral transcendence which is located in the higher rational capacities inherent in any individual human being. It is the latter element in the analysis which leads organic communitarian and post-modern critics to identify critical theory as another version of cosmopolitanism. According to this critique, the problem with critical theory is that it is insufficiently ontologically and epistemologically radical in its analysis of the self of self-determination which is crucial to its emancipatory project, the human individual. For communitarians, this is a matter of the underestimation of the inherently social nature of the self and the contextual determination of moral claims (Walzer 1983; 1994a). For post-modernists, it is a matter of the volatility of any ontological categorisation and the unsustainability of any normative theoretical high ground (Walker 1993; 1999; Jahn 1998).

Post-modernism, like critical theory, challenges the idea that nations and states have any particular normative status or right to autonomy. In the case of critical theory, this challenge rests on an analysis of international politics in which nations and states form elements of a complex totality which transcends them, a totality which includes, crucially, the moral capital immanent in modern universalism. In the case of post-modernism, this challenge rests on a similar reconceptualisation of international politics in which boundaries between inside and outside are understood as fluid, permeable and capable of being transgressed. However, for post-modernism, first, the inside-outside boundaries which constitute the autonomous individual are included in the challenge and, second, the idea of moral capital inherent in modern universalism is rejected (Ashley and Walker 1990; Walker 1993; Devetak 1996; Ashley 1996; Campbell 1998a; 1998b; Dillon 1998).

Post-modernism substitutes subject positions for subjects and multiple, discursively constructed identity or identities for any given cultural identity or identities. In post-modernism there is no prior-existing self, whether naturally, morally or culturally constituted, which exists to ground the right of self-determination. The ethic of post-modernism shifts discourses based on a linkage between rights and the given ontological categories of individuals, nations and states toward a discourse of process and achievement. However, even though identities of all kinds are treated as volatile constructions, it is the achievement of agency by identities which are disempowered by dominant forms of political identity which are given a normatively exemplary status in post-modernist theory (Ashley and Walker 1990). The tendency of dominant strands of both normative and explanatory theory in international politics to treat certain identities as fixed and beyond question is seen to be not only ontologically mistaken, but also normatively wrong (Campbell 1998a: 513–4; 1998b: 163). In general, because of post-modernism's rejection of both Kantian and communitarian conceptions of the individual as well as their rejections of the necessity of the dominance of nations and states as modes of political organisation, post-modernism valorises the work of international actors which challenges any or all of these given limitations. The idea of self-determination understood as a categorical imperative to respect and acknowledge responsibility toward the 'other' operates as a regulative ideal in post-modernists' normative assessments of various kinds of political struggle in contemporary international politics (Campbell 1998a: 513). This leads to a focus on and implicit prescriptive endorsement of a politics and ethics of difference:

> Much of the postmodern turn can be understood as a series of attempts to reclaim or reconstruct or even to finally create some practical space for, say, a Kantian concern with the conditions of

> the possibility of knowledge or the meaning of autonomy in a
> world in which the secular guarantees of Reason and History can
> no longer console us for the death of God. It can also be
> understood as a multi-faceted struggle to come to terms with the
> possibility of a critical or emancipatory political practice given
> the extent to which the great secular substitutes for God in
> modern political thought – Reason, History, the sovereign state,
> the sovereign individual and the universal class – have themselves
> come to seem so problematic. (Walker 1993: 20.)

Thus, for post-modernism, the question of whether there is a right to
national self-determination makes no sense in general, because it
assumes a given content both to the category of nation and the
category of self-determination. Nevertheless, it is clear that in certain
contexts, post-modernists might well want to argue for the positive
normative significance of struggles for rights to nationhood or the sub-
state recognition of national identity and, indeed, for any other aspect
of identity which has been constructed in opposition to the given,
dominant limitations (Campbell 1998a: 513). However, it is also clear
that for post-modernists the judgement necessarily shifts once a
particular mode of political agency comes into a dominant position,
either through its exclusion of other nascent identities externally or its
limitation of its own dynamic possibilities internally. This is nicely
illustrated in some post-modernist reaction to feminist theory and
politics. Post-modernists are sympathetic to feminist politics up to the
point at which it relies on fixed understandings of the categories of
women or gender, then it (feminism) becomes condemned for its
imperialist imposition of particular forms of gendered identity on all
women (Walker 1988: 151).

It should be apparent, therefore, that in one sense post-modernism
endorses the notion that all moral obligations are 'special'. Such
obligations are always the product of specific and complex conditions.
Nevertheless, in contrast to communitarianism (with which there
appears initially to be considerable prescriptive overlap), post-
modernism's relativism is twinned with a positive endorsement of the
general value of difference and resistance over identity and
government. It is this general endorsement which underlies the nature
of the contextual judgement which post-modernist theorists make
about actual political struggles. This is why both multiculturalism
within states and the rights of refugees and migrants against states tend
to be supported, or even given exemplary status, by post-modernist

theory. This is not simply because post-modernists such as Walker see this kind of politics as an aspect of the ontological realities of the emerging global order, but also because the opening up of possibilities for alternative identities to flourish and the opening up of state borders is in accord with the normative status given to the transgression of limits by post-modernists in both theory and practice. It is this generalised commitment to ongoing deconstruction and the enabling of difference as both theoretical practice and practical prescription that leads other schools of normative theory engaging with the question of rights to self-determination to see post-modernism as rendering normative debate in international relations meaningless. In fact, however, it is this commitment which makes post-modernism most easily recognisable as normative theory in a traditional sense, one which pits an ideal of eternal overcoming in a 'first best' world against a second-best world and always already finds the latter wanting (Campbell 1998b: 219).

Feminist international theory takes a variety of forms, and there is no single feminist response to traditional questions about rights to self-determination in an international context. As with liberal nationalists and critical theorists, however, feminism does not generally give inherent value to nations and states as autonomous entities. Both nations and states are valued only in so far as they empower or disempower those affected by gendered relations of power.[4] This suggests that feminism shares with liberal nationalism and critical theory a fundamental attachment to the concept of individual autonomy. However, feminists are also critical of the idea of individual self-determination underlying dominant liberal discourses, such as those of international human rights. This is because it is argued that the notion of 'individual' or 'human' with which such discourses operate is blind to the significance of sexual difference or gendered identity (MacKinnon 1993). As Spike Peterson suggests:

> the discourse and practice of international human rights retains a male-as-norm orientation that persists in treating women's rights as secondary.

> International human rights conventions specifically reject the principle of non-intervention when violation of rights occur. Yet systematic violence against women is treated as 'customary' or a 'private matter', and thus immune to international condemnation. (Spike Peterson 1990: 305.)

What does this criticism imply for feminist normative engagement with the concept of self-determination? It can be taken as an argument that the ideal of self-determination is the same for all human beings, but that existing human rights regimes omit, or pay insufficient attention to, specific ways in which women's rights need to be protected in a patriarchal world (liberal feminism). On this account, the aim of feminist politics is to produce the conditions within which women can be sovereign individuals in a classically liberal-contractarian or Kantian sense. It can also be taken as an argument for the need to develop a norm of specifically female self-determination, against which struggles for individual, national or state autonomy could be judged (radical feminism). It is this kind of view which underlies the notion of sex-differentiated citizenship rights and feminist challenges to rights of nations or states to exploit or oppress women (Elshtain 1981; Pateman 1988; 1992; MacKinnon 1993). In much feminist theory, however, including Spike Peterson's work cited above, the argument against liberal rights discourses implies a more radical challenge to the concept of individual self-determination, one which calls into question the notion of individuals (generic or gendered) as either ideally or really the same kinds of independent entity as each other (difference feminism). The implication of this kind of feminist theoretical approach is to extend the undermining of inside-outside distinctions between different subjects of self-determination which characterises critical theory and post-modernism to women as well as individuals, nations and states (Bock and James 1992; Steans 1998: 60–80).

These three different kinds of feminist theoretical response can be seen at work in arguments within feminism about the right to national self-determination and the sub-state recognition of cultural identity. For liberal feminists, such rights are dependent on the extent to which equality of rights for women are institutionalised within any given political community. Liberal feminism, therefore, takes a similar normative position to liberal statism and liberal nationalism in judging collective right essentially in terms of individual right. Radical feminism charges liberal feminism with misunderstanding the essentially masculine nature of a supposedly generic model of autonomy. In its place, radical feminism sets gendered identity against generic concepts of individual self-determination and gives it normative priority over national and state right, so that neither established cultural value nor a community 'general will' are recognised as valid subjects of self-determination as such. Difference feminism has been developed as a response to both liberal and sexual-difference feminisms by feminists who have identified themselves as simultaneously subject to gendered relations of power and excluded by mainstream feminist accounts of what women's right to self-determination means. In particular, difference feminism has objected to the notion of 'women as such' and, in ways which parallel communitarian and post-modernist arguments, argued that suggesting a fixed identity for all women conceals the cultural imperialism of white against non-white and western against non-western women (Mohanty *et al.* 1991; Marchand and Parpart 1995; Yuval-Davis 1998). Difference feminism revives the possibility of the normative significance of nation and culture as subjects of self-determination. In some versions, it essentially repeats communitarian and post-modernist conceptions and evaluations of cultural relativism. However, it can also be interpreted in a way which, in spite of the parallels, is subtly different from the arguments of communitarians and post-modernists. As against communitarianism, difference feminism treats inside-outside, national-cultural boundaries as inherently permeable, so that while it assumes the possibility and value of identification of women with nation or community, it also assumes the possibility and value of identification of women with other women across national or cultural boundaries. Commonality of condition is not a matter of 'either-or' choices or a normative hierarchy of right – both overlaps and clashes between national and gendered selves as subjects of self-determination are an ongoing matter of contingency. As against post-modernism, difference feminism does not work on the presumption of an ideal of self-determination as the transgression of given limitation. Instead, the ideal is located within the fluid, but also sticky, possibilities available. Of all of the perspectives considered so far, difference feminism is the one which has paid most attention to the impossibility of disentangling self from other determination (and identity) in the quest for criteria by which to judge the value of different kinds of political struggle (Hutchings 1999).

Normative Judgement Beyond Deconstruction

Critical theory, post-modernism, radical and difference feminisms deconstruct the self-contained subjects of self-determination in cosmopolitan and communitarian ethics of international politics. In doing this, they, as it were, confront the first-best ideal world with the second-best actuality in which there is no purity of individual or collective self or self-will. Self-determination is always also other determination in a context in which the conditions of possibility of agency are necessarily heteronomous. For this reason, these kinds of critical approaches avoid the perpetual battle, characteristic of liberal and communitarian debates, to make different sorts of self-determination compatible which have already been defined in incompatible terms. However, it is still unclear what lessons follow for normative theorising from the deconstructive work carried out by critical, post-modernist and feminist theorists. In particular, what are the implications for assessing claims made as to the rightness or wrongness of particular normative responses to questions of individual, national or state right? A standard response from more orthodox ethical perspectives to the approaches discussed above is to raise the question, if there is no place for the validation of judgement beyond the complexities of the second-best world, then how do you validate the judgement that, for example, female circumcision is wrong and persuade others of its truth? In what follows, I attempt to articulate the kind of normative theoretical response which is derivable from these deconstructive approaches in relation to the ethical question of whether cultures which deny women individual rights to self-determination should be ethically condemned.

In terms of mainstream normative theory, the positions taken on this issue have generally approximated to familiar cosmopolitan and communitarian alternatives, with the former regarding 'traditional' cultures as fundamentally disrespectful of women's right to individual self-determination and the latter stressing that the nature and validity of women's rights depend on the overarching value system or systems operative within their (women's) communities, communities which have an inherent right to be respected. The exchange between these ethical positions follows an equally familiar pattern, with universalist and particularist moral ontologies, objectivist and relativist moral epistemologies set against each other, but with the idea of self-determination crucial to both. From the point of view of critical international theories, for this argument to become something more than a slanging match between ethical universalism and ethical particularism, three stages of theoretical work are necessary. The first stage involves the, by now familiar, process of putting into question the categories and assumptions through which the question as to the universal validity of claims for women's rights is posed. The second stage involves accounting for the prescriptive agendas of those who are putting, or responding to, the question. The third involves the utilisation of resources examined in the previous stages to support a specific prescriptive position.

The first stage of analysis is not intended to settle the question of right and wrong, but to establish the extent to which right and wrong are actually in question. The condemnation of community in the name of individual right relies on a world-view in which both individuals and communities are conceptualised as self-contained units. As demonstrated in the previous section, such a world-view relies on an untenable first-best understanding of the nature of individuals and collectives which is, therefore, necessarily blind to the complexities of meaning of which the second-best world is capable. The significance of the different ways of valuing and treating women for women in different contexts is not obvious once the radical disjunction between individual and collective self-determination is called into question. For instance, it may become apparent that abortion rights are necessarily linked to enforced female infanticide in some contexts and to enhanced life chances for women in others, or that the politics of female circumcision are fundamentally bound up with religious or nationalist affiliations which affect its priority as an issue for women in some contexts, whereas it is a key site for emancipatory struggle in others. In other words, the question of what self-determination means cannot be settled in advance of what it is recognised to mean in the real, second-best world. This is not to say that ethical clashes in the understanding of the meaning and value of self-determination for women in the second-best world will not emerge. But by taking seriously the impossibility of disentangling self from other-determination at either an individual or collective level, normative analysis is much less likely to make the mistake of mapping ethical differences onto taken-for-granted distinctions between individual and community, which then enable the mutual demonisation of incompatible ethical positions.

Deconstructing the terms in which the question of the condemnation of communities which do not respect the rights of women is put does not answer the question. Instead, it suggests the prescriptive agenda of a variety of ways in which the question is asked and the inevitable implication of these agendas in how it is answered. Accounting for such agendas is the second stage of normative theoretical work implied by critical international theories. At this stage, the task of the theorist is to articulate the fullest possible account of the meaning of self-determination implicit in the asking and answering of the question. This articulation must include both the grounds and implications of the claim being made. For those arguing, for instance, for a liberal position, the range of legal, social, political and economic conditions which both underpin and are implied by a liberal understanding of the meaning of individual self-determination must be made clear. But part of this clarification must also be to point up what is lost as well as what is gained from the identification of women as 'persons' and the internal tensions within liberal states between the recognition of women as persons and their positioning in relation to the public/private distinction. This exercise is not going to resolve the question of whether women are entitled to rights of abortion or over their own body in an absolute sense. But normative theory can make explicit how it already has been, can be, or could be institutionalised and what may be lost or gained in the process.

The third stage of theoretical work implicit in critical normative approaches is required when the theorist moves beyond the deconstruction and analysis of given normative judgements to the formulation of his or her own version of questions and answers about rights to self-determination. However, it is the two previous stages of analysis which provide the resources and clarify the limitations of any such formulation and which provide the basis for the judgement of the validity of the prescriptive agenda being put forward. If a normative theorist judges, for instance, that women should have rights over their own bodies it is incumbent upon him or her to make explicit both the grounding of that judgement in his or her place in the second-best world and the nature of the (desired) world in which such a prescription makes sense. There is no security of authority in normative judgement and it is always partial and exclusive. But to the extent that such judgement is open about its own conditionality and exclusivity, it can form part of an ongoing argument and struggle toward the conditions of possibility of the recognition of the validity of that judgement by others. The truth of normative judgement does not rely on short cuts provided by access to epistemic authority, neither does it rely on argument or rhetoric alone, rather it relies on the capacity of others to identify with the premises which underpin and the promises which follow from any particular normative claim. When mainstream approaches to normative theory ask the critical theorist to respond to questions such as whether female circumcision is wrong, the critical theorist is obliged to answer that this depends on the world you inhabit and desire to inhabit. The task of demonstrating that a world should be constructed in which it is obvious that female circumcision is wrong itself depends on elements of that world being sufficiently in place for the claim to make sense to those who are listening. Without such elements, prescription must rely not on argument but on coercion.

Conclusion

It might be expected that by beginning with the mutual interconnection of the different possible subjects of self-determination in international politics, rather than their ideal insulation, critical international theories would avoid the displacement of their own criteria of judgement into the transcendent realm of what ought to be the case. However, the rethinking of the subjects of self-determination (individual, nation and state) carried through by the critical theories does not necessarily imply the rejection of an ideal of self-determination which operates over the actual conditions of possibility of agency. In critical theory, the ideal reappears expressed in terms of the Habermasian conditions of non-distorted communication; in post-modernism, it reappears as the general imperative to deconstruct or reconstruct the given limits of political agency and identity; in some versions of feminism, it reappears as sex-differentiated rights for women. In essence, the more or less residual presence of traditional ideals of self-determination in the normative judgements of critical theory, post-modernism and feminism reflects the survival of the idea of autonomous as opposed to heteronomous determination and categorical as opposed to hypothetical ethical imperatives. In critical theory's 'transcendence', post-modernism's 'transgression' and feminism's vision of women's self-determination, the same model of pure natural or rational self-creation which is crucial to liberalism's grounding of individual right and communitarianism's grounding of collective right is to be found. It is this tendency toward theoretical purity which helps to fuel traditional realist charges as to the irrelevance and dangerous implications of normative judgement as such in the realm of international politics.

However, the tendency toward slippage back into the terms of old idealist-realist or cosmopolitan-communitarian debates is counteracted by the equally significant tendency in critical international theories toward a new kind of realism. According to this version of realism, a normative judgement is not unrealistic (utopian or idealistic) because it presents a vision of a different kind of world. It is only unrealistic (utopian or idealistic) if it fails to engage with the conditions of possibility of the new world in relation to the old by taking a short cut through an idealised ontology in which pure self-determination is possible and an idealised epistemology in which normative judgements are authorised by transcendent authority. According to this view, it is dangerous to treat any model of self-determination as a generic ideal, however formal, to provide criteria for judgements of right and wrong – not because such models may not be genuinely inspiring and meaningful ideals, but because they invariably involve, but rarely acknowledge, specific cultural and political conditions of possibility by which they were enabled and in relation to which they make sense. This problematises claims to the generalisability in principle of particular ideals and it also draws attention to the fact that attempts to realise such ideals will have radically different consequences in different contexts, but at the same time it keeps in place recognition of the unavoidability of making normative claims and the difficulties surrounding their realisation.

NOTES

1. In this tradition of thought, individual rights are conceived largely in 'negative' terms of the protection of individuals against encroachments on their freedom by the state and law. Thus protection of bodily integrity and property rights has a particularly high priority (Cranston 1973). Mapel (1992) provides an overview of liberal contractarian thinking in international theory and certain examples are discussed below (Steiner 1992; Charvet 1996). See O'Neill (1991; 1992) for a critical perspective on liberal contractarianism from a liberal Kantian viewpoint.

2. The key difference between Kantian and contractarian approaches and those of utilitarianism and Marxism to issues of human rights is that the first two perspectives link the idea of rights to a strong notion of the intrinsic value of individual autonomy, whereas for the latter two the notion of rights is of instrumental value only in relation to broader general goals. In the case of Marxism, the whole notion of individual rights is a suspect one: rights discourses are, at best, a way of ameliorating conditions in an imperfect world which needs to be changed much more fundamentally (Brown 1992; Nielsen 1998).

3. I am using the term 'deconstruction' here in a non-Derridean, technical sense to signify the taking apart and reconstructing of the concepts of self and self-determination at work in the theoretical work considered in the previous section.

4. The tensions between feminist politics and nationalist politics have been the subject of considerable debate in feminist literature, see Charles and Hintjens (1998). There is also a very considerable literature on feminism and citizenship rights; for an overview, see Hutchings (1999).

REFERENCES

Ashley, R., 1996. The achievements of post-structuralism. In *International Theory: Positivism and Beyond*, ed. Smith, S., Booth, K. and Zalewski, M. Cambridge, Cambridge University Press.

Ashley, R.K. and Walker, R.J.B. 1990. Reading dissidence/writing the discipline: crisis and the question of sovereignty in international studies. *International Studies Quarterly*, Vol.34, No.3, pp.367–416.

Barry, B. and Goodin, R., eds. 1992, *Free Movement: Ethical Issues in the Transnational Migration of People and Money*. London: Harvester Wheatsheaf.

Beetham, D., ed. 1995. Politics and human rights. *Political Studies*, Vol.43, special issue.
Bock, G. and James, S., eds. 1992, *Beyond Equality and Difference: Citizenship, Feminist Politics and Female Subjectivity*. London: Routledge.
Brown, C. 1992, *International Relations Theory: New Normative Approaches*. Hemel Hempstead: Harvester Wheatsheaf.
Campbell, D. 1998a. Why fight: humanitarianism, principles and post-structuralism. *Millennium*, Vol.27, No.3, pp.497–521.
        1998b, *National Deconstruction: Violence, Identity and Justice in Bosnia*. Minneapolis and London: University of Minnesota Press.
Campbell, D. and Dillon, M., eds. 1993, *The Political Subject of Violence*. Manchester: Manchester University Press.
Caney, S., 1996. Individuals, nations and obligations. In *National Rights, International Obligations*, ed. Caney *et al*. Boulder (CO), Westview.
Caney, S., George, D. and Jones, P., eds. 1996, *National Rights, International Obligations*. Boulder (CO): Westview.
Canovan, M. 1996a, *Nationhood and Political Theory*. Cheltenham: Edward Elgar.
        1996b. The skeleton in the cupboard: nationhood, patriotism and limited loyalties. In *National Rights, International Obligations*, ed. Caney *et al*. Boulder (CO), Westview.
Charles, N. and Hintjens, H. 1998, *Gender, Ethnicity and Political Ideologies*. London: Routledge.
Charvet, J., 1996. What is nationality, and is there a moral right to national self-determination? In *National Rights, International Obligations*, ed. Caney *et al*. Boulder (CO), Westview.
Cranston, M. 1973, *What Are Human Rights?* New York: Taplinger.
Devetak, R., 1996. Postmodernism. In *Theories of International Relations*, ed. Burchill, S. and Linklater, A. London, Macmillan.
Dillon, M. 1998. Criminalising social and political violence internationally. *Millennium*, Vol.27, No.3, pp.543–67.
Elshtain, J.B. 1981, *Public Man/Private Woman: Women in Social and Political Thought*. Princeton: Princeton University Press.
Falk, R. 1995, *On Humane Governance*. Cambridge: Polity.
George, D., 1996. National identity and national self-determination. In *National Rights, International Obligations*, ed. Caney *et al*. Boulder (CO), Westview.
Gilbert, P., 1996. National obligations: political, cultural or societal? In *National Rights, International Obligations*, ed. Caney *et al*. Boulder (CO), Westview.
        1998, *The Philosophy of Nationalism*. Boulder (CO): Westview Press.
Habermas, J. 1990, *Moral Consciousness and Communicative Action*. Cambridge: Polity Press.
Hoffman, M., 1993. Agency, identity and intervention. In *Political Theory, International Relations and the Ethics of Intervention*, ed. Forbes, I. and Hoffman, M. London, Macmillan.
Hutchings, K., 1999. Feminist politics and cosmopolitan citizenship. In *Cosmopolitan Citizenship*, eds. Hutchings, K. and Dannreuther, R. London, Macmillan.
        1999, *International Political Theory: Re-thinking Ethics in a Global Era*. London: Sage.
Hutchings, K. and Dannreuther, R., eds. 1999, *Cosmopolitan Citizenship*. London: Macmillan.
Jahn, B. 1998. One step forward, two steps back: critical theory as the latest edition of liberal idealism. *Millennium*, Vol.27, No.3, pp.613–41.
Kant, I. 1991, *The Metaphysics of Morals*. Cambridge: Cambridge University Press.
Kymlicka, W. 1995, *Multicultural Citizenship*. Oxford: Clarendon.
Linklater, A. 1998, *The Transformation of Political Community*. Cambridge: Polity.

1999. Cosmopolitan citizenship. In *Cosmopolitan Citizenship*, eds. Hutchings, K. and Dannreuther, R. London, Macmillan.

MacCormick, N., 1996. What place for nationalism in the modern world? In *National Rights, International Obligations*, ed. Caney et al. Boulder (CO), Westview.

MacKinnon, C., 1993. Crimes of war, crimes of peace. In *On Human Rights: The Oxford Amnesty Lectures 1993*, eds. Shute, S. and Hurley, S. New York, Basic Books.

Mapel, D., 1992. The contractarian tradition and international ethics. In *Traditions of International Ethics*, eds. Nardin, T. and Mapel, D. Cambridge, Cambridge University Press.

Marchand, M.H. and Parpart, J.L., eds. 1995, *Feminism, Postmodernism, Development*. London: Routledge.

Miller, D. 1995, *On Nationality*. Oxford: Clarendon Press.

1999. Bounded citizenship. In *Cosmopolitan Citizenship*, eds. Hutchings, K. and Dannreuther, R. London, Macmillan.

Mohanty, C., Russo, A. and Torres, L., eds. 1991, *Third World Women and the Politics of Feminism*. Bloomington and Indianapolis: Indiana University Press.

Nardin, T. and Mapel, D., eds. 1992, *Traditions of International Ethics*. Cambridge: Cambridge University Press.

Nickel, J.W. 1987, *Making Sense of Human Rights*. Berkeley: University of California Press.

Nielsen, K. 1998. Is global justice impossible? Res Publica, Vol.4, No.2, pp.131–66.

O'Neill, O., 1991. Transnational justice. In *Political Theory Today*, ed. Held, D. Cambridge, Polity.

1992. Commentary: magic associations and imperfect people. In *Free Movement: Ethical Issues in the Transnational Migration of People and Money*, eds. Barry, B. and Goodin, R. London, Harvester Wheatsheaf.

Pateman, C. 1988, *The Sexual Contract*. Cambridge: Polity.

1992. Equality, difference, subordination: the politics of motherhood and women's citizenship. In *Beyond Equality and Difference: Citizenship, Feminist Politics and Female Subjectivity*, eds. Bock, G. and James, S. London, Routledge.

Shue, H. 1996, *Basic Rights: Subsistence, Affluence and US Foreign Policy*, second edition. Princeton (NJ): Princeton University Press.

Spike Peterson, V. 1990. Whose rights? A critique of the 'givens' in human rights discourse. *Alternatives*, Vol.15, pp.303–44.

Steans, J. 1998, *Gender and International Relations*. Cambridge: Polity.

Steiner, H., 1992. Libertarianism and the transnational migration of people. In *Free Movement: Ethical Issues in the Transnational Migration of People and Money*, eds. Barry, B. and Goodin, R. London, Harvester Wheatsheaf.

1996. Territorial justice. In *National Rights, International Obligations*, ed. Caney et al. Boulder (CO), Westview.

Tamir, Y. 1993, *Liberal Nationalism*. Princeton (NJ): Princeton University Press.

1996. Reconstructing the landscape of imagination. In *National Rights, International Obligations*, ed. Caney et al. Boulder (CO), Westview.

Vincent, R.J., 1992. The idea of rights in international ethics. In *Traditions of International Ethics*, eds. Nardin, T. and Mapel, D. Cambridge, Cambridge University Press.

Walker, R.B.J. 1988, *One World, Many Worlds: Struggles for Just World Peace*. Boulder (CO): Lynne Reiner.

1993, *Inside/Outside: International Relations as a Political Theory*. Cambridge: Cambridge University Press.

1999. Citizenship after the modern subject. In *Cosmopolitan Citizenship*, eds. Hutchings, K. and Dannreuther, R. London, Macmillan.

Walzer, M., 1981. The distribution of membership. In *Boundaries: National Autonomy and Its Limits*, eds. Brown, P.G. and Shue, H. Totowa (NJ), Rowman & Littlefield.

1983, *Spheres of Justice: a Defence of Pluralism and Equality*. Oxford: Blackwell.
1992, *Just and Unjust Wars*, second edition. New York: Basic Books.
1994a, *Thick and Thin: Moral Argument at Home and Abroad*. Notre Dame: University of Notre Dame Press.
1994b. Notes on the new tribalism. In *Political Restructuring in Europe: Ethical Perspectives*, ed. Brown, C. London, Routledge.
Yuval-Davis, N., 1998. Beyond differences: women, empowerment and coalition politics. In *Gender, Ethnicity and Political Ideologies*, eds. Charles, N. and Hintjens, H. London, Routledge.

7

Derrida and the Heidegger Controversy: Global Friendship Against Racism

MARK BEVIR

In 1989, Victor Farias's *Heidegger and Nazism* appeared in English translation, thereby bringing to prominence over here what has become known as the Heidegger controversy. Martin Heidegger joined the National Socialist Party on 1 May 1933, remained a paying member throughout the war, and at times seemed to express enthusiastic support for the Nazis. Farias went on to argue that Heidegger's involvement with Nazism was profound, deep, and lasting. Although some scholars applauded Farias's work, others, including Jacques Derrida, denounced it as excessive and distorted. Of great concern was the apparently unforgivable silence of Heidegger after the war: not once did he condemn without equivocation the Holocaust. In one article, Derrida interprets this silence as 'an honest' admission by Heidegger that he could not respond adequately to what had happened (Derrida 1990: 148). Derrida's interpretation can seem appallingly generous given that the silence was over a moral condemnation of Auschwitz not a philosophical problem. Some commentators even suggested that this appalling generosity indicated a sort of complicity in Nazism on the part of deconstruction.

Elsewhere, however, Derrida has treated Heidegger's politics at much greater length. In *Of Spirit: Heidegger and the Question*, first published in French in 1987, Derrida, with the insight and rigour characteristic of his deconstructive practice, follows the place of 'spirit' and spirit in Heidegger's work. 'Could it be', he asks, that from 1927 to 1953 Heidegger 'forgot to avoid?' (Derrida 1989: 2).[1] Did Heidegger avow a metaphysical concept of spirit that implicated his philosophy in Nazism? Derrida's reflections on 'Heidegger and the Question' open up numerous avenues of inquiry. I want to follow an avenue that will lead us to the ethics of deconstruction. More particularly, I hope to highlight a 'cosmopolitan' moment within deconstruction, a moment that can be obscured by the prominence given therein to identity, difference, and alterity. If we forget to avoid metaphysics, we are in danger of following Heidegger in reifying nations, cultures, or groups in a way which entails a spiritual racism, a hostility to the Other. To avoid the particularism of spiritual racism, we need a non-metaphysical 'cosmopolitanism' that supports a suitable openness to alterity. A non-metaphysical 'cosmopolitanism' differs from the liberal universalism that underlines most contemporary defences of global norms. It should be understood as an ethical stance of friendship to the Other, rather than an agreed set of principles or rights.

Derrida's reading of Heidegger highlights the presence within our response to Nazism of a philosophical problem as well as a need for moral condemnation. He draws out uncomfortable overlaps between the biological racism of the Nazis, the spiritual racism of Heidegger, and the metaphysical thinking informing much of our universalism. By doing so, he returns us to our 'cosmopolitan' responsibilities.

'Spirit' and Spirit

Heidegger set out initially to use phenomenology to explore the nature of Being (Heidegger 1962). Like Edmund Husserl, he wanted to break out of a dichotomy of subject and object so as to return to an original experience. Unlike Husserl, however, he identified this original experience with our being in the world, not our consciousness. For Heidegger, our lived experience provided the route to Being because we alone can experience Being as a question. By holding ourselves open to this question, to our being, we can approach Being itself. In Heidegger's later writings, usually understood to commence with the 'Letter on Humanism', he turned from this phenomenological analysis of lived experience to an attempt to recover Being by escaping metaphysics through studies of language and history (Heidegger 1978: 189–242). We do not find Being in our own existence; rather, Being reveals itself to us through language – we should listen to language to hear what Being has to tell us. Throughout Heidegger's life, he sought to make Being once again a question for us. Spirit represented for him 'the determined resolve to the essence of Being, a resolve that is attuned to origins and knowing' (Heidegger 1993a: 33). Spirit is the posing of the question of Being whether through our lived experience or through language, history, and the overcoming of metaphysics.

In *Of Spirit*, Derrida seeks 'to recognise in' Heidegger's understanding of spirit (*Geist*) an 'equivocation or indecision, the edging or dividing path which ought, according to Heidegger, to pass between a Greek or Christian – even onto-theological – determination of *pneuma* or *spiritus*, and a thinking of *Geist* which would be other and more originary' (Derrida 1989: 82). In *Being and Time*, Heidegger defines spirit principally as what it is not: not a substance, not the thing in itself. He argues that if we understand spirit in terms of the presence of our being, we get caught up in questions of the *cogito*, and so fail once again to raise the question of Being. Heidegger thus opens up a distinction between spirit defined positively in relation to the *cogito* or our being, a concept he rejects, and 'spirit' defined negatively in relation to the question of Being, a concept he endorses. As Derrida comments, Heidegger introduces spirit as something to be avoided, while endorsing 'spirit' almost as if he were borrowing the former word for other uses. 'Spirit' is said to contain the truth of Being, but in many ways it seems to act more as a mark of the absence of spirit. What is Derrida pointing to here? At the risk of making the relevant issues and distinctions too simple and clear cut, we might contrast two interpretations or uses of 'spirit'. If 'spirit' becomes the site of a positive truth, it is reified; it becomes a metaphysical or onto-theological concept akin to spirit – perhaps it even becomes a postulated answer to the question. Alternatively, we might think of 'spirit' as a radical absence, a concept placed under erasure as are so many of the terms in Derrida's lexicon. If we did this, 'spirit' would point to just those forms of non-metaphysical thinking that have preoccupied Derrida, and also Heidegger in his later writings.

Derrida, in a characteristic deconstructive gesture, attempts less to resolve these two interpretations of Heidegger's use of 'spirit' than to show how they coexist in tension. For Derrida, one of the features of reading Heidegger is that in doing so we are 'aware of both these vibrations at the same time' (Derrida 1989: 68).2§ Nonetheless, it would not be wildly inaccurate to say that Derrida reads the metaphysical concept of 'spirit' as dominant in Heidegger's Rectoral Address of 1933 and his *An Introduction to Metaphysics* of 1935, with the non-metaphysical one appearing most prominently in Heidegger's later writings, notably the essay on Georg Trakl, 'Language in the Poem' (Heidegger 1993a; 1959; 1971). Although we should not reduce complex shifts in Heidegger's politics to equally complex ones in his philosophy, the implication is clear: Heidegger's involvement with the National Socialist Party coincided with his reliance on a concept of 'spirit' that forgets to avoid metaphysics.

Spirit and Racism

Heidegger's use of spirit to convey the truth of Being leads, if not inexorably then with a certain force, to a metaphysical entanglement with a concept of the *Volk* that is dangerously close to that of the National Socialists. Derrida traces this process in Heidegger's infamous Rectoral Address of 1933, 'The Self-Assertion of the German University'. It is in this text that we find the definition of spirit already given: spirit is 'the determined resolve to the essence of Being'. According to Derrida, the Rectoral Address derives its momentum from this positive concept of spirit. Self-assertion requires, even consists of, a more or less conscious affirmation of the spiritual mission. To be fully human, we have to embrace spirit. Fully to assert our human being, we have to pose the question of Being. Heidegger then associates the particular German character of the university with such an affirmation of the spiritual mission. A *Volk*, he argues, has a spiritual world, where the power of this world reflects the strength of its embrace of spirit, that is, the language and history through which its people approach Being. The ideal, developed, spiritual world thus 'comes from preserving at the most profound level the forces that are rooted in the soil and blood of a *Volk*, the power to arouse most inwardly and to shake most extensively the *Volk*'s existence' (Heidegger 1993a: 33–4). For Heidegger, such 'a spiritual world alone will guarantee our *Volk* greatness' (Heidegger 1993a: 34).

Derrida traces the same approach to spirit in Heidegger's *Introduction to Metaphysics*. Here Heidegger explicitly stands back from any particular politics in order to stress the importance of Being-resolute. What really matters, he implies, is that we should hold ourselves correctly; we should open ourselves to Being; we should affirm the spiritual mission. The particular direction of our being is of little moment compared to such Being-resolute. In addition, Heidegger expresses regret at what he sees as a decadence of spirit. He calls vigorously for greater resoluteness, a renewed focus on the spiritual mission, and a return to the question of Being. Once again, moreover, Heidegger equates such a renewal with a strengthening of the particular spiritual world of the German people.

According to Derrida, Heidegger is guilty in these texts of 'both evils'; namely, 'the sanctioning of Nazism, and the gesture that is still metaphysical' (Derrida 1989: 40). Heidegger adopted a positive concept of spirit, not an absent 'spirit', and so an equally positive ideal of the spiritual mission which then underlay his relationship with the

Nazis. On the one hand, Heidegger committed himself to the National Socialist Party on the grounds that it embodied an aspiration toward a powerful spiritual *Volk*. On the other hand, he tried to overcome what he saw as shortcomings in National Socialism by 'spiritualising' the movement and thus turning its ideology from a biology of race to the question of Being (Derrida 1989: 39).

Heidegger himself later tried to distinguish sharply between his evocation of a spiritual world and the Nazi's biologism of race. As he explained to the Rector of Freiburg University in a letter dated 4 November 1945: 'it sufficed for me to express my fundamental philosophical positions against the dogmatism and primitivism of Rosenberg's biologism'; 'I sought to show that language was not the biological-racial essence of man, but conversely, that the essence of man was based in language as a basic reality of *spirit*.' (Heidegger 1993b: 64.) Derrida spends considerable time in *Of Spirit* questioning the force of this distinction. He suggests that Heidegger's entanglement with metaphysics does not overcome racism so much as displace it from biology to spirit. Heidegger ascribes the responsibility for the spiritual mission to the German people. He argues, as Derrida explains, that to 'awaken spirit', to call 'it back to the care of the question of Being', is 'the historical mission of *our people*' (Derrida 1989: 67). In particular, Heidegger ties the fate of spirit to that of the German language. The German people and their language alone can produce Being out of our being.³ Surely, however, this spiritual elevation of a particular people contains a racial gesture? As Derrida pertinently remarks, 'the *German* character of this university is not a secondary or contingent predicate, it cannot be dissociated from this affirmation of spirit' (Derrida 1989: 33). Surely, therefore, Heidegger like the Nazis proclaimed the greatness of the German *Volk*, albeit that he did so by moving from spirit to race and even biology rather than from biology to race and even spirit. Yet, as Derrida pertinently asks: 'by thus inverting the direction of determination, is Heidegger alleviating or aggravating this "thought of race"? Is a metaphysics of race more or less serious than a naturalism or a biologism of race?' (Derrida 1989: 74.)

Derrida finds a link between Heidegger's spiritual racism and his forgetting to put spirit under erasure. Heidegger constantly strove to avoid metaphysics in both his early and later writings. Yet from 1934 to 1945 he in some sense forgot to hold himself open to Being and perhaps therefore became entangled in both metaphysics and National Socialism. To follow Derrida this far is to raise at least two sets of questions. The first concerns the dangers of metaphysics. What is it about a metaphysical concept of spirit that raises the spectre of racism? What does Derrida's reading of Heidegger tell us we should be wary of? The second set of questions concerns the possibility of avoiding not only the biological racism of the Nazis, but also the spiritual racism of Heidegger. Did Heidegger have to take a metaphysical turn to oppose the extreme horrors of Nazism? Is there a non-metaphysical thinking that avoids spiritual as well as biological racism?

Racism and Cosmopolitanism

What is it about a metaphysical concept of spirit that raises the spectre of racism? I believe that Derrida highlights the danger of postulating any fixed identity, no matter how loosely defined, as the basis of a group, nation, or race. We need always to question, and thus deconstruct, any such fixed identity. We must not follow Heidegger in evoking a spiritual mission or any other positive content as the basis of any group whatsoever. Instead, we must always remain open and responsible to the Other. In *Of Spirit*, Derrida highlights these things by insisting that language is prior to the question of Being. Heidegger, at least from 1934 to 1945, seems to have begun with the question of Being as the basis for a metaphysical concept of spirit. The priority of the question of Being enabled him to define a positive spiritual mission in terms of an engagement with this question so that the acceptance of this mission then could become a possible basis for the self-assertion of the German people. Derrida, in contrast, insists that there is 'language always, *before any question*' (Derrida 1989: 94). Language stands here for 'the promise' that 'has already taken place wherever language comes' – 'a sort of promise of originary alliance to which we must have in some sense already acquiesced, already said *yes*, given a pledge' (Derrida 1989: 94, 129). A promise of alliance, a responsibility to the Other, an openness to alterity – all of these things come before any positive concept of spirit, even one based on a question. As Derrida explains elsewhere, 'to respond' is to be 'caught, surprised (*pris, surpris*) in a certain responsibility'; 'we are invested with an undeniable responsibility at the moment we begin to signify something', where 'this responsibility assigns us our freedom' – 'it is assigned to us by the Other' (Derrida 1988a: 634). Before all things, we have a moral responsibility that puts us in a relationship to the Other. Before any allegiance to a particular group, we belong to a cosmopolitan community.

Derrida's critique of Heidegger's concept of spirit points to a distinction between two ways of invoking the other. On the one hand, Heidegger introduces an existential concept of the other as a positive presence in the individual's life. The other stands for those with whom we build an inherently shared life-world. It stands for people with whom we share an identity, or perhaps people with whom we are engaged in a common enterprise. On the other hand, Derrida's work introduces an ethical concept of the Other as the logical possibility of someone, even something, absent from the individual's life. The Other stands for those who might be found beyond our life-world. It reminds us of people who do not share a particular identity, who are not engaged in a particular enterprise, but to whom we still have a moral responsibility. It evokes 'a *we* which is perhaps not *given*' (Derrida 1989: 107).

According to Heidegger, we cannot know ourselves or address the question of Being except in relation to others defined as those with whom we share a world. 'Knowing oneself is grounded in Being-with', he tells us; 'it operates proximally in accordance with the kind of Being which is closest to us – Being-in-the-world as Being-with; and it does so by an acquaintance with that which *Dasein*, along with the Others, comes across in its environmental circumspection' (Heidegger 1962: 161). Others are conceived here in terms of their proximity to our being. They are those who, through their relations with us, help to create our world, our Being-there. For Heidegger, moreover, our ethical relationship with these others arises out of just this proximity. 'The Other is proximally disclosed', he explains, 'in concernful solicitude' since 'solicitous concern is understood in terms of what we are concerned with' (Heidegger 1962: 161).

Derrida suggests that because Heidegger's existential concept of the other relies on proximity, it embodies a particular identity or enterprise in a way that raises the spectre of racism. According to Derrida, our concept of the Other should exceed that found in Heidegger. Although we have our being only in common with those others with whom we share a life-world, there is an Other that comes 'before' our existential relationship to these others. In a move typical of deconstruction, Derrida argues that the presence of Heideggerian others always entails an absent Other. Even as we recognise the importance of others in constructing our life-world, so we inevitably open the space of the Other understood as that which remains outside of the shared life-world we thus evoke. To forget this Other is to adopt a metaphysical standpoint that raises the spectre of racism. We have to exhibit a cosmopolitan openness to the Other as well as a solicitous concern for others.

The concept of the Other sets up a cosmopolitan responsibility prior to any commitment to a shared identity or common enterprise. Hence Derrida has often insisted that there is 'no ethics without the presence of the other' (Derrida 1977: 139–40). Several features of his thought stand for cosmopolitanism against the particularism represented, here, by Heidegger's focus on others at the expense of the Other. Derrida's attacks on the idea of a finite, stable individual reflect a belief that our being is always a being with others. Yet his insistence on the importance of difference (of recognising how any present is bound up with an absent) entails a stress on the inherent limitations of all attempts to postulate a particular culture as that which binds us to the relevant others. Consider, for example, the notion that the self is constituted by a particular culture or community; perhaps religion is integral to the identity of Muslims, or maybe gender defines interests shared by all women, or perhaps Native Americans acquire certain beliefs and practices from their race. Derrida's emphasis on difference undermines such particularism: it points to the possibility of deconstructing such reified identities to recover the multiple, complex, even indeterminate identities adopted by Muslims, women, and Native Americans. Consider also the notion that a culture or community is defined by certain beliefs and practices; perhaps people are Christians only if they act in a required fashion, or maybe true men have to be heterosexual, or perhaps the German *Volk* is defined by its unique relationship to the spiritual mission. Derrida's emphasis on difference again undermines such particularism: it points to the possibility of deconstructing such reified cultures to reveal the multiple, complex, even indeterminate beliefs and practises adopted by Christians, men, or Germans.

For Derrida, any attempt to reify a culture as that which binds us to others involves the sort of metaphysics and racism he finds in much of Heidegger's work. To reify a culture is to set up an apparently simple presence without recognising the place of what is absent; it is to force the fact of difference into a myth of sameness; it is to collapse the ethical Other into existential others. To avoid the particularism associated with such a reification of groups or cultures, we must adopt a cosmopolitanism that remains open to the ethical Other. We must respect singularity in a way that asks of us an openness to alterity. We must acknowledge an ethical relationship prior to our membership of any particular group, a relationship that does not depend upon the other holding certain beliefs, recognising given authorities, performing a set of actions, belonging to a particular race, living in a certain neighbourhood, or speaking a given language. To avoid metaphysical thinking and spiritual racism, we have constantly to remember our ethical responsibility to the Other.

Cosmopolitanism and 'Spirit'

Is there a non-metaphysical thinking that avoids spiritual as well as biological racism? Derrida suggests that Heidegger's metaphysical use of spirit was intimately connected with his spiritual racism. Yet within Heidegger's writings, he argues, we also find a non-metaphysical concept of 'spirit'. 'Spirit' clearly stands, here, for the non-metaphysical type of thinking that Derrida has tried to reveal through his practice of deconstruction. His study of the place of 'spirit' in Heidegger's thought thus runs parallel to his more general concern to avoid the logocentrism he finds throughout the western philosophical tradition.

After 1945, Heidegger moved away from the metaphysical concept of spirit toward that of 'spirit'. Even in his *Introduction to Metaphysics*, he had argued that the question had to be prior to any metaphysics since a metaphysical position would constitute not only an orientation toward the question, but also a posing of a question. This argument suggests that there might be a notion of spirit as an original 'yes' which comes before even the question of Being. There might be a moment of ethical freedom or obligation underlying the very possibility of questioning. At the time, however, Heidegger's entanglement with a metaphysical concept of spirit led him to a spiritual racism rather than a pursuit of this moment of obligation. Many of Heidegger's later works, such as 'The Question Concerning Technology', also seem to prioritise questioning or thinking over an original 'yes'. Yet Derrida highlights a subtle shift, particularly in the 1953 study of Trakl, 'Language in the Poem', which takes Heidegger from questioning to listening to the promise of language (Heidegger 1977; 1971).

For the later Heidegger, spirit, the pursuit of the question of Being, is not first; it is not something that falls into or governs space and time. Rather, the posing of the question of Being now presupposes that language has already been given to us. Thus Heidegger comes to emphasise the importance of listening to the pledge of language. All questioning relies on the fact that language already has been given to us. Crucially, Derrida adds, this means that an ethical space opens up in relation to language, an ethical space that is prior to the question of Being. The possibility of the question, of ontology, of philosophy, all these possibilities occur within the space of language, that is, of a responsibility to the Other within a cosmopolitan community. The question 'answers in advance' to a 'pledge'; 'it is engaged by it [this pledge] in a responsibility it has not chosen and which assigns it even its liberty' (Derrida 1989: 130). Ethics enters into our thinking at the very moment that thinking begins.

According to Derrida, when Heidegger thus placed ethics before ontology, he moved away from a logocentrism found not only in his own earlier work, but also in 'the whole European and Christian-metaphysical discourse which holds to the word *geistig* instead of thinking the *geistliche* in the sense supposedly given it by Trakl' (Derrida 1989: 101). Heidegger's recognition of an original 'yes' enables us to begin a more appropriate non-metaphysical thinking of 'spirit'. One of the ways in which Derrida approaches this non-metaphysical concept of 'spirit' is through an imaginary dialogue between Heidegger and some Christian theologians. The theologians press Heidegger on the similarities between his originary understanding of 'spirit' and a radical Christian metaphysics. In what surely must be a key passage in *Of Spirit*, Heidegger replies: '*Geist* is not first of all this, that, or the other.' Rather:

> It is indeed not a new content. But access to thought, the thinking access to the *possibility* of metaphysics or pneumato-spiritualist religions opens onto something quite other than what the possibility makes possible. It opens on to what remains *origin-heterogeneous*. What you represent as a simply ontological and transcendental replica is quite other. This is why, without opposing myself to that of which I am trying to think the most matutinal possibility, without even using words other than those of the tradition, I follow the path of a repetition which crosses the path of the entirely other. The entirely other announces itself in the most rigorous repetition. And this repetition is also the most vertiginous and the most abyssal (Derrida 1989: 112–3).[4]

'Spirit' is first of all the mark of an absent heterogeneity that is problematically forced to become a homogenous presence within metaphysical thinking. Heidegger wants to insist on the importance of remaining open to this heterogeneity even as one becomes embroiled in the terminology of traditional metaphysics. Although he continues to use the word spirit, he does so while recognising a responsibility to the entirely Other who would fall beyond any simple ontological designation of the word spirit, a responsibility one might denote by placing scare-quotes around the word, thus 'spirit'. Interestingly, Derrida has the Christian theologians agree with Heidegger. 'Yes,' they say, 'that's just what we're saying.' (Derrida 1989: 113.) Their metaphysics contains within it the possibility of approaching an anti-metaphysical recognition of the original pledge. Similarly, Heidegger's non-metaphysical thinking does not totally avoid traditional metaphysics so much as carry within it traces of such metaphysics. 'Spirit' cannot avoid spirit. It stands not as a discrete alternative to tradition so much as a reminder of heterogeneity. It does not evoke an alternative positive content, but rather a responsibility to the Other.

I want to pause here to highlight some key moments of Derrida's non-metaphysical thinking as they appear in his reading of Heidegger. The first moment of Derridean thought is its embodiment of an ethical demand. Deconstruction has been portrayed as a form of nihilism celebrating the free play of signifiers and texts without offering any criteria of judgement. In contrast, we have found that deconstruction insists on the priority of ethics over ontology. It introduces the notion of an original responsibility to the Other. The second moment of Derridean thought is a critique of traditional metaphysics for failing to recognise this responsibility. Derrida's detailed works of deconstruction neither follow random chains of signifiers nor unpack insignificant marginal contradictions within texts. They highlight those places where authors, texts, philosophy, the tradition, and disciplines all fail to allow for alterity and so become exclusionary and imperialistic. The third moment of Derridean thought is an acceptance of the impossibility of our standing outside of metaphysics. As soon as we pose a question, we enter a realm of speech or thought in which we necessarily impose a certain homogeneity upon difference. Deconstruction does not seek to transcend such a realm, but rather to work within it so as to prevent our forgetting that we are responding to an original promise and to remind us of the responsibility this promise entails. The final moment of Derridean thought is the way concepts are put under erasure or placed within scare-quotes. This way of treating concepts highlights both the fact that metaphysical thinking always carries within it the traces of a forgotten absence and the fact that non-metaphysical thinking cannot avoid setting up homogenous categories.

'Spirit' and 'Cosmopolitanism'

Derridean thought is characterised by its persistent return to an ethical demand prior to ontology. Heidegger's writings exhibited a spiritual racism precisely because he forgot to respect alterity when he adopted a metaphysical concept of spirit. Suitably to remember the Other is to adopt a cosmopolitanism free from the particularism that characterises spiritual as well as biological racism. Yet Derrida constantly emphasises that our responsibility to the Other entails a non-metaphysical form of thinking in which concepts are put under erasure. Perhaps, therefore, we should evoke a 'cosmopolitanism' rather than cosmopolitanism. By doing so, we would highlight the differences between the non-metaphysical 'cosmopolitanism' found in Derrida's work and the metaphysical universalism that is so common among liberals. Derrida, as I have read him, has much in common with liberal universalists: he highlights the instability of cultures and so the problems of individuating them; he reveals the dangers inherent in the reification of cultures; and he consequently calls for a global openness in which the different individual, not the different culture, is the unit of concern. Nonetheless, from a Derridean perspective liberal universalism remains unacceptably wedded to a metaphysics of presence. Derrida's 'cosmopolitan' concern with our responsibility to the Other stands apart from a liberal concern with rules and rights in that it rigorously seeks to avoid a logic of the same, a logic perilously close to the metaphysical concept of spirit associated with Heidegger's racism.

In contrasting a Derridean 'cosmopolitanism' with a liberal universalism, I am likely to open myself to the criticism that I rely on a simplistic account of the liberal position. Liberals might argue that their position does not necessarily entail a logic of the same, a metaphysics of presence, a commitment to neutrality, or a particular notion of reasonableness. To some extent such criticisms and arguments would be about words alone with nothing of substance being at stake: if two people agreed, what would it matter whether they saw themselves as liberals or Derrideans? Nonetheless, it is worth briefly considering these criticisms and arguments since liberal attempts to accommodate a Derridean position would be likely to exemplify precisely that ethos that distinguishes their universalism from 'cosmopolitanism'. So, on the one hand, perhaps I will offer a caricature of liberalism – undoubtedly, I will ignore the subtleties, complexities, and vacillations found in the work of many liberals. On the other hand, I will do so partly in opposition to the imperialistic nature of a liberalism that often seeks to define a consensus such that its critics are represented as liberals and so pressurised to accept certain terms of debate. Such an imperialistic liberalism characteristically remains unaware of, let alone apologetic for, the way in which it thereby excludes or belittles important aspects of the identity of the critics it claims to accommodate.

Much liberalism remains wedded to individualism.[5] The individual is conceived as being autonomous, that is, as being at least capable of standing in splendid isolation outside of society. Derrida, in contrast, is well known for his opposition to the 'fantasmatic organisation' of the 'finite individual' (Derrida 1984: 118). Like Heidegger, Derrida always insists that our being is a being with others. At the very least, he insists that we can have a relation to self only where we have relations to others, and often he also suggests that even then we cannot have any real relation to self. Just as Heidegger argues that the presence of the other provides the necessary context for questioning, so Derrida relies on the presence of the Other to establish the ethical moment that comes before ontology. The responsibility and freedom of this ethical moment are 'assigned to us by the Other, from the Other, before any hope of reappropriation permits us to assume this responsibility in the space of what could be called *autonomy*' (Derrida 1988a: 634). In this sense, we share with others an 'absolute past' that brings us 'together in a sort of minimal community' (Derrida 1988a: 636). Where Derrida differs from Heidegger is in his denial that a particular identity, shared mission, or any other presence can act as the basis of this community. Because any 'we' 'tries its luck' within a culture or tradition that is not 'homogenous', 'our principal concern will be to recognise the major marks of a tension within it, perhaps even ruptures, in any case, scansions' (Derrida 1988a: 634–5). Derrida rejects Heidegger's particularism, with its spiritual racism, for an open 'cosmopolitanism' that deliberately avoids even implicitly setting up any criteria by which we might demarcate members of the community.

Because liberals generally are wedded to individualism, they tend to adopt a universalism based on a vision of how individuals should come together. They postulate a set of rights that individuals, or perhaps cultures, acquire by virtue of entering global society, or they explore the global norms on which all individuals, or perhaps cultures, can agree. Liberal universalism concerns the rights of individuals and groups within global society conceived as an organisation, that is, as a collectivity formed by individuals or groups in pursuit of a specific end, such as peace, order, or social justice. Derridean 'cosmopolitanism', in contrast, begins with a recognition of the fact that individuals have their being only in relation to one another. It does not consist of agreed norms or a set of rights so much as a reminder of the ethical stance or responsibility to others that follows from this fact of community. This responsibility moves us from an artificial, even imperialistic, construction of consensus, or agreed norms, to an openness to alterity. It moves us from a duty of respecting the rights of others to a gift of friendship to the Other.

Liberal universalism typically poses as a neutral position, one upon which all reasonable people can agree. In doing so, however, it reifies the cosmopolitan community in much the same way as Heidegger did the *Volk*. Liberal universalism bases the cosmopolitan community on a fixed identity defined by this neutral position. From a Derridean perspective, therefore, liberal universalism is insufficiently attuned to difference. It does not allow for people who do not share the allegedly neutral position upon which it is based. Either liberal universalism is imperialistic in that it includes the Other in a consensus to which it does not belong or it is exclusionary in that it dismisses the Other as unreasonable. The scare-quotes around 'cosmopolitanism', in contrast, serve to make explicit an acceptance of an undecidable moment in the ethic we affirm. 'Cosmopolitanism' admits to non-neutrality. Although we should respect 'cosmopolitanism', and although, in a gesture that is neither wholly strategic nor yet essential, we must at any moment give positive content to this 'cosmopolitanism', we always should respect the element of chance, 'the strange violence', that inevitably is embedded in this positive content (Derrida 1988a: 634). 'Cosmopolitanism' is defiantly provisional and perpetually haunted by the ghost of the very metaphysics of spirit that it seeks to avoid. It welcomes the call constantly to interrogate our norms in the name of the Other.

Because liberals do not adequately recognise the undecided nature of cosmopolitanism, they are too quick to tie it down to a particular content. Typically, this content consists of a particular set of rights acquired by individuals or cultures as they enter global society. 'Cosmopolitanism', in contrast, evokes, in Derrida's words, a minimal community that is located in an absolute past conceived as 'pure passivity preceding liberty' and so comes before legal obligations and rights (Derrida 1988a: 636). It requires of us less an acceptance of moral rules than a certain type of ethical conduct. It calls us to a practice of friendship within which people would open themselves to one another in an attempt to grant to the others those things that are deemed essential for flourishing. The practice of friendship requires a 'respect of the Other' that 'maintains the absolute singularity of the Other' even as it 'passes through the universality of the law'; thus, we can ask not only 'Does not my relation to the singularity of the Other as Other pass through the law?' but also 'Does not the law command me to recognise the transcendent alterity of the Other who can only ever be heterogeneous and singular, hence resistant to the very generality of the law?' (Derrida 1988a: 640–1.) We should offer a generous hospitality to that Other whom liberals so often dismiss as unreasonable and we should keep a place open for that Other whom liberals so often dismiss as absent.

'Cosmopolitanism' and Deconstruction

Farias's exploration of Heidegger's relationship to Nazism occurred at much the same time as the discovery of Paul de Man's connections with National Socialism (de Man 1988; Wiener 1991).[6] Several commentators used this conjunction as an excuse to challenge the ethical credentials of the philosophy and textual practice of deconstruction. Jurgen Habermas denounced deconstruction as an irrationalist anti-modernism that belonged alongside the German conservatism of the 1920s and 1930s (Habermas 1987; 1989). This tradition of irrationalist conservatism had been broken after the Third Reich, but Derrida's work is providing a temptation, even an excuse, to resurrect it. Deconstruction stood charged, at best, with being apolitical, inspiring quietism or even nihilism and, at worse, with being intimately connected with Fascism. Before long, several voices came to Derrida's defence. Simon Critchley, in particular, emphasised the relationship between Derrida's work and that of Emmanuel Levinas so as to demonstrate the ethical responsibilities demanded by deconstruction (Critchley 1992). Clearly, one purpose of my arguments has been to reinforce Critchley's position. The philosophy of deconstruction points to an ethical moment of responsibility to the Other that is prior to ontology, and this moment informs the type of non-metaphysical thinking found in Derrida's textual practice. In addition, I have tried to unpack this ethical moment, somewhat differently from Critchley, as a 'cosmopolitanism' predicated on a minimal community and an openness to alterity.

Yet the debate on the ethics of deconstruction did not end there. The year after the appearance of Critchley's defence of deconstruction, Richard Wolin published a scathing attack on Derrida's response to the

Heidegger controversy (Wolin 1993). Wolin was angered by Derrida's refusal to allow his article, 'Philosophers' Hell', to be reprinted in further editions of a selection of essays edited by Wolin even though it already had appeared in the first edition. Wolin interpreted this refusal as 'an act of self-criticism', that is, an attempt by Derrida to distance himself from 'a quasi-exoneration of Heidegger's philosophically overdetermined commitment to National Socialism' (Wolin 1993: xii). Perhaps some of Derrida's comments did not do sufficient justice to the horrors of Nazism. Surely though, any intemperance in Derrida's tone is more than matched by Wolin's description of this as a 'quasi-exoneration' of a commitment to Nazism? Putting such intemperance to one side, however, we should recognise that Wolin raises an important issue. He says, 'what is especially troubling about Derrida's text (and one might make the same observations about his book on the subject, *Of Spirit: Heidegger and the Question*) is that the "foundational" deconstructive gesture of overturning and reinscription ends up by threatening to efface many of the essential differences between Nazism and non-Nazism' (Wolin 1993: xiii).

Of course we should denounce National Socialism clearly and unequivocally. Derrida certainly does so: 'I have always condemned Nazism.' (Derrida 1984: 8.) We can do this, however, with or without insisting on an absolute break between National Socialism and all other forms of thinking. Derrida's reading of Heidegger does indeed draw our attention to similarities between biological racism and spiritual racism and between spiritual racism and metaphysical thinking. He suggests that Heidegger's metaphysics of the spirit does not totally avoid racism, but rather displaces the question of race from biology to spirit. Wolin raises the question: is Derrida right to relate Heidegger's Nazism to a politics of spirit that even today people wish to deploy against the inhuman? Much of my discussion has been designed to show why Derrida does just this. Derrida alerts us to the place of racism, or a lack of recognition of Otherness, throughout our philosophical tradition. Properly to understand the appeal of Nazism to Heidegger is also to be sensitive to certain moral dangers that we confront. The practice of deconstruction prompts us to remember and to avoid these dangers.

Ultimately, what is at stake in Derrida's critique of Heidegger is whether we can dismiss National Socialism as a mere irrational aberration. The issue is not whether we should condemn Fascism (of course we should), but whether we should wholeheartedly embrace the legacy of the Enlightenment. Liberal universalists such as Habermas and Wolin think that we can: Nazism embodied a biological racism entirely alien to the universalist spirit of the Enlightenment. Derrida suggests that we cannot: biological racism has uncomfortable similarities with a spiritual racism associated with a form of metaphysical thinking found not only in Heidegger but also in liberal universalism. While we are still compelled to defend a 'cosmopolitan' position, we should be careful all the while to remember, always to remember, our responsibility to the Other.

NOTES

1. In many ways, *Of Spirit* continues Derrida's recurring exploration of the place of spirit in modern idealism, and especially Hegel (Derrida 1986a).
2. Derrida briefly lists places in Heidegger's work where 'signs and markers' of the later non-metaphysical concept of 'spirit' might be traced (Derrida 1989: 133).
3. Derrida unpacks Heidegger's position thus: 'German is ... the only language, at the end of the day, at the end of the race, to be able to name this maximal or superlative [spirit].' (Derrida 1989: 71.)
4. Earlier Derrida unpacks this vital notion of the origin-heterogeneous: '*Origin-heterogeneous*: this is to be understood at once, all at once in three senses: (1) heterogeneous from the origin, originally heterogeneous; (2) heterogeneous with respect to what is called the origin, other than the origin and irreducible to it; (3) heterogeneous *and* or *insofar as* at the origin, origin-heterogeneous because at the origin of the origin.' (Derrida 1989: 107–8.)
5. Much of what follows runs parallel to the dispute between liberals and communitarians (Mulhall and Swift 1992). Derrida shares the communitarian critique of the thin, liberal self, while refusing to follow them, as well as Heidegger, in postulating a fixed identity as the basis of a discrete community.
6. Derrida has responded to the de Man affair (Derrida 1986b; 1988b).

REFERENCES

Critchley, S. 1992, *The Ethics of Deconstruction: Derrida and Levinas*. Oxford: Blackwell.
de Man, P. 1988, *Wartime Journalism, 1939–1943*. Lincoln: University of Nebraska Press.
Derrida, J. 1977, *Of Grammatology*, trans. Spivak, G. Baltimore: Johns Hopkins Press.
    1984, *Signéponge/Signsponge*, trans. Rand, R. New York: Columbia University Press.
    1986a, *Glas*, trans. Leavey, J. Jr. and Rand, R. Lincoln: University of Nebraska Press.
    1986b, *Memoires for Paul de Man*. New York: Columbia University Press.
    1988a. The politics of friendship. *Journal of Philosophy*, Vol.85, No.11, pp.632–44.
    1988b. Like the sound of the sea deep within a shell: Paul de Man's war. *Critical Inquiry*, Vol.14, No.3, pp.590–652.
    1989, *Of Spirit: Heidegger and the Question*, trans. Bennington, G. and Bowlby, R. Chicago: University of Chicago Press.
    1990. Heidegger's silence. In *Martin Heidegger and National Socialism: Questions and Answers*, eds. Neske, G. and Kettering, E. New York, Paragon House.
Farias, V. 1989, *Heidegger and Nazism*. Philadelphia: Temple University Press.

Habermas, J. 1987, *The Philosophical Discourse of Modernity*, trans. Lawrence, F. Cambridge (MA): MIT Press.

1989. Work und Weltanschauung: the Heidegger controversy from a German perspective. *Critical Inquiry*, Vol.15, No.2, pp.431–56.

Heidegger, M. 1959, *An Introduction to Metaphysics*. New Haven: Yale University Press.

1962, *Being and Time*, trans. Macquarrie, J. and Robinson, E. London: SCM Press.

1971. Language and the poem: a discussion on Georg Trakl's poetic work. In *On the Way to Language*. New York, Harper & Row.

1977. The question concerning technology. In *The Question Concerning Technology and Other Essays*, trans. Lovitt, W. New York, Harper & Row.

1978. Letter on humanism. In *Basic Readings*, ed. Knell, D. London, Routledge & Kegan Paul.

1993a. The self-assertion of the German University. In *The Heidegger Controversy: A Critical Reader*, ed. Wolin, R. Cambridge (MA), MIT Press.

1993b. Letter to the rector of Freiburg University, 4 November 1945. In *The Heidegger Controversy: A Critical Reader*, ed. Wolin, R. Cambridge (MA), MIT Press.

Mulhall, S. and Swift, A. 1992, *Liberals and Communitarians*. Oxford: Basil Blackwell.

Wiener, J. 1991, *Professors, Politics and Pop*. London: Verso.

Wolin, R., 1993. Preface to the MIT Press edition: Note on a missing text. In *The Heidegger Controversy: A Critical Reader*, ed. Wolin, R. Cambridge (MA), MIT Press.

8

Humanitarian Vigilantes or Legal Entrepreneurs: Enforcing Human Rights in International Society

NICHOLAS J. WHEELER

'Those who took the law into their own hands had never improved civic peace within nations; neither would they help in international relations', declared the Indian ambassador to the Security Council during its debate on the legality of NATO's bombing of the Federal Republic of Yugoslavia (FRY). India's objections were strongly supported by Russia and China who argued that NATO was acting illegally because the Security Council had not expressly authorised the action. Although the leading governments prosecuting the war against the Milošević regime claimed that they had legal authority for their action, they conceded that their use of force lacked explicit authorisation from the Security Council. Yet, since the latter is the only body in international society that is authorised to mandate the use of force for purposes other than self-defence, a key question raised by NATO's war in Kosovo is the implications it has for the UN system of maintaining international peace and security.

The fundamental problem raised by intervention in Kosovo was that the society of states had two of its settled norms at loggerheads with each other (Frost 1996). On the one hand, since 1945 states have recognised a growing commitment to uphold internationally agreed standards of human rights. The way in which a government treats its

An earlier version of this article was presented to the colloquium on 'Global Norms and Diverse Cultures' held at the University of Newcastle in January 1999. I would like to thank all those who took part for their helpful comments on my paper. My thinking on this subject was greatly enriched by conversations with Chris Brown and Andrew Linklater. Alex Bellamy and Emily Haslam provided many valuable comments and Maja Zehfuss translated some key speeches made in the German Bundestag. I am also grateful to Tim Dunne for helping me to think more creatively about the relationship between norms and law in international society, and for his incisive comments on earlier drafts of the article.

own citizens is now a legitimate matter of international scrutiny on the part of governments and human rights non-governmental organisations (NGOs) such as Amnesty International and Human Rights Watch. On the other hand, the society of states has not developed enforcement mechanisms for ensuring compliance with global humanitarian norms. The Security Council can authorise intervention under Chapter VII of the UN Charter for the purpose of maintaining 'international peace and security'. During the 1990s, it has employed this power, with varying degrees of success, to protect human rights in successive post-cold-war humanitarian crises. However, there is no norm enabling states to intervene for humanitarian purposes in the absence of express Security Council authorisation, and no state or group of states has tried to advance such a norm in post-1945 international society. The significance, then, of NATO's use of force in Kosovo is that a group of states have employed force without express Security Council authorisation and justified it on explicitly humanitarian grounds.[1] The question is whether such a development is to be welcomed or feared in a society of states built on the principles of sovereignty, non-intervention and non-use of force. Is NATO's attempt at promoting justice in Kosovo placing at risk the foundations of international order, or does it presage the beginnings of a new doctrine of humanitarian intervention in which the society of states bestows upon particular states, or groups of states, the legal right to use force to protect internationally agreed standards of human rights?

Hedley Bull referred to the collective capacity to assure compliance with human rights standards as signifying the existence of a solidarist international society. A solidarist international society, he argued, was one in which there is a 'solidarity ... of the states comprising international society, with respect to the enforcement of the law'[2] (Bull 1966: 52). Writing in 1966, Bull thought that this conception of international society was premature, but more than three decades later, is Bull's verdict still relevant? The problem with Bull's conception of solidarism is that he gives us no criteria by which to measure this. Consequently, he is vulnerable to the challenge that Chris Brown has recently directed against the theory of international society, namely, that it does not provide a theory of agency when it comes to the question of how global norms are to be enforced (Brown 1999: 15). 'Under what circumstances', Brown asks, 'is [enforcement] action to be seen as the action of "international society" and not simply of the individual states who take it?' (Brown 1999: 11–12.) The answer that

I want to pursue here in relation to the Kosovo case is that the litmus test of whether states are acting as agents of international society is the extent to which their actions secure collective legitimation.

To explore how far NATO secured international legitimacy for its intervention in Kosovo, the article draws upon three models for thinking about the question of collective legitimation in international society: the posse, the vigilante, and the norm entrepreneur.[3] The idea of the posse is taken from the 'wild west' and refers to a situation where the sheriff calls upon the assistance of a group of citizens to assist him in the task of law enforcement. These individuals are given a warrant to use force from the sheriff and are accountable to him for their actions. The response of the UN Security Council to humanitarian crises in Somalia, Bosnia and Rwanda fits the model of the posse in that the Security Council explicitly authorised member states under Chapter VII to act on its behalf to secure humanitarian objectives. However, Kosovo does not conform to posse action as the lack of unanimity among the permanent members led to a situation in which NATO could not secure a warrant for military action from the Security Council. This is where the idea of an international equivalent to the vigilante comes in. The term vigilante, as Chris Brown points out, developed in the USA in the nineteenth century and explains the actions of those private individuals who enforced the law in the absence or breakdown of officially constituted legal bodies. The key point about vigilantes is that they claim to be enforcing agreed law on behalf of the community; they do not advance new norms nor do they try to create new law (Brown 1999: 12). No one has legally authorised NATO to act in Kosovo, but Alliance governments claim, as do contemporary vigilantes in domestic society, to be acting with the authority of the law.

Thinking about NATO's action in Kosovo in terms of vigilantism is at first sight an appealing interpretation. The Security Council as the legally constituted law-enforcement body failed to act and NATO stepped in to enforce the Security Council's writ. This view suits Alliance governments who want to argue that their action did not break international law and upheld human rights values in the society of states. However, there is an alternative reading of NATO's action that would emphasise how far some members of the Alliance, notably the Blair government, were advancing new norms in justifying the use of force in Kosovo. Martha Finnemore and Kathryn Sikkink argue that the development of new norms depends crucially upon particular states acting as 'norm entrepreneurs' who attempt to convince other states to

embrace the norm (Finnemore and Sikkink 1998: 895). There follows
a process of contestation as the advocates of the new norm try to
persuade a critical mass of followers that their action should not be
viewed as an example of norm-breaking behaviour. If the norm
entrepreneur succeeds in gaining a large group of supporters, then
Finnemore and Sikkink argue that a 'norm cascade' takes place as the
new standard of appropriate behaviour becomes internalised by actors.
Lastly, there is the 'internalisation' phase where the norm becomes part
of the taken-for-granted understandings and is no longer the subject of
contestation (Finnemore and Sikkink 1998: 895–905). If Alliance
governments acted as 'norm entrepreneurs' in Kosovo, then the new
norm that is being raised is the legal right of states to use force to
defend human rights without express Security Council authorisation.
Finnemore and Sikkink consider that a fruitful area for future research
is to investigate which norms become law, suggesting that successful
entrepreneurs will create new laws. With this question in mind, the
article asks how far NATO has played the role of a 'legal entrepreneur'
in Kosovo by setting a precedent for a new customary law supporting
the legality of humanitarian intervention.

Although governments during the cold war never pressed the
argument for a right of humanitarian intervention, a small group of
international lawyers championed this case. The first part of the article
sets out this legal argument and briefly shows how it secured little or
no support in state practice during the cold war. Here, I identify two
key reasons as to why states were so reluctant to embrace a legal rule
of humanitarian intervention. The next part of the article considers the
legal arguments raised by Alliance governments for their use of force
in Kosovo, and lastly, I examine how far the international response to
the humanitarian claims raised by NATO indicate a change in state
practice on the legality of humanitarian intervention. How many states
have to embrace the new norm before it can be said to have secured
legitimacy, and what are the implications for the creation of new law if
Russia, China and India remain outside of any emerging consensus?

The Legality of Humanitarian Intervention During the Cold War

The legal argument in defence of a right of humanitarian intervention
rests on two bases: an interpretation of UN Charter provisions relating
to the protection of human rights and customary international law.
Most international lawyers argue that the prohibition in Article 2 (4)
against the use of force renders humanitarian intervention by

individual states illegal. The only exception to this general ban on the use of force is the right of self-defence under Article 51. However, a minority of lawyers argue that the promotion of human rights should rank alongside peace and security in the hierarchy of Charter principles. Here, they point to the language in the Preamble of the Charter which talks about 'faith in fundamental human rights' and the obligations set out in Article 1 (3) and Articles 55 and 56 of the Charter, which require members to take 'joint and separate action in co-operation with the Organisation' to promote human rights. According to Fernando Teson, the 'promotion of human rights is as important a purpose in the Charter as is the control of international conflict' (Teson 1988: 131). Consequently, Teson argues that the UN Security Council has a responsibility to promote human rights and that it should exercise its Chapter VII enforcement powers to this end.

For legal interventionists, the ban in Article 2 (7) on Security Council intervention in 'matters which are essentially within the domestic jurisdiction' of states should not apply in cases of massive human rights violations because this is a matter of international concern.[4] Moreover, it follows from this that if the Security Council fails to take corrective action to prevent or halt human rights abuses, then individual states should take the law into their own hands and act as vigilantes to enforce human rights by the threat or use of force. Michael Reisman and Mryes McDougal claim that were this not the case, 'it would be suicidally destructive of the explicit purposes for which the United Nations was established' (Reisman and McDougal quoted in Arend and Beck 1993: 133). Thus, for these lawyers explicit Security Council authorisation under Chapter VII is not necessary to legalise acts of humanitarian intervention since the existence of human rights norms requires that individual states act as law enforcers of the humanitarian purposes embodied in the UN Charter.

This case for a legal right of humanitarian intervention under UN Charter law is buttressed by the claim that prior to the UN Charter there existed a right in customary international law which continues to function in the post-Charter environment. For states to consider themselves bound by a rule of customary international law, there must be two key elements: state practice and *opinio juris*. It is not enough to point to state practice since this only becomes transformed into a binding rule of international law if the actors believe that this practice is required by the law. I will come back to the difficulties of deciding when a new custom has arisen when I discuss the Kosovo case later, but for the moment, there are two responses that can be made against the contention that there already exists a customary rule of humanitarian intervention. The first is that while there are cases in the nineteenth century where European states invoked a legal right of humanitarian intervention to rescue persecuted Christian minorities in the Ottoman Empire, none of these interventions occurred in a context where the intervening states and target state viewed themselves as equal and legitimate members of a common international society. As Franck and Rodley put it, interventions against Turkey reflected 'relations between unequal states ... in which "civilised" states exercise *de facto* tutorial rights over "uncivilised" ones' (Franck and Rodley 1974: 278–9). Second, in the post-1945 context, there have been cases where a government is committing mass murder against its citizens and where there have been interventions by neighbouring states which led to the ending of the human rights abuses. I am thinking here of India's use of force against East Pakistan in 1971, Vietnam's intervention against Cambodia in December 1978 and Tanzania's intervention a few months later against Uganda. If these states believed that a customary law of humanitarian intervention existed, then how are we to explain the fact that none of them justified their actions in terms of a legal right of humanitarian intervention? Moreover, the condemnation that greeted India, and especially Vietnam's use of force, indicates that other states did not think that humanitarian intervention was acceptable in the cold war.[5]

How, then, should we explain the reluctance of states to embrace a doctrine of humanitarian intervention, and how far do these reasons persist at the end of the cold war? Pluralist international society theorists would argue that it reflects an appreciation of the value of the order provided by the rules of sovereignty and non-intervention. Hedley Bull accepted that the practices of the society of states generate terrible moral conflicts between order and justice, and considered that in deciding between the two it was necessary to bear two considerations in mind: the consequences for international order of any attempt to promote justice and the degree of injustice embodied in the existing order. Humanitarian intervention is the archetypal case where it might be expected that international society would decide to recognise legally an exception to its cardinal rules. However, Bull argued in 1984 that the society of states had not legitimised practices of humanitarian intervention because of fears that giving such a legal right to particular states would 'jeopardise the rules of sovereignty and non-intervention' (Bull 1984: 193). The pluralist concern is that humanitarian intervention should not be permitted in the absence of a consensus on what moral principles should govern a practice of humanitarian intervention. To concede such a right to individual states in the absence of any such agreement is to open the door to powerful states acting on their own particular moral preferences, thereby weakening the restraints on the recourse to force in the society of states.

For pluralists, then, the problem is not who is to be entrusted with enforcing the will of an embryonic solidarist society of states; rather, they question whether there exists the normative consensus to enforce even basic standards of international humanitarian law. The problem is not that states do not recognise the existence of these standards, since they constitute a shared language within which states argue over the rights and wrongs of particular cases. However, this shared language does not resolve the problem of what to do when states disagree over which rule to apply in particular cases, or whether a particular action is in conformity with a shared rule. For example, there might be general agreement that the 1948 Convention Against the Crime of Genocide permits humanitarian intervention, but pluralists argue that culturally diverse states with conflicting interests cannot be expected to agree in particular cases whether a situation should be named as a genocide.

Realists share with pluralists the suspicion that humanitarian intervention will always be based on the 'cultural predilections of those with the power to carry it out' (Brown 1992: 113). However, they introduce a further objection which is that any legal right of humanitarian intervention will always be open to abuse. The problem of abuse only arises in a context where humanitarian justifications for the use of force have secured an important measure of collective legitimation. The concern is that by permitting a further exception to that of self-defence in Article 2 (4) of the UN Charter, states will be free to abuse this new legal right by claiming humanitarian justifications to cover the use of force motivated by selfish interests. The international lawyer Ian Brownlie (who represented the FRY when it tried unsuccessfully in April 1999 to persuade the International Court of Justice (ICJ) to decide that NATO's bombing was illegal) relates the problem of abuse specifically to vigilante action:

> Whatever special cases one can point to, a rule allowing humanitarian intervention, as opposed to a discretion in the United Nations to act through the appropriate organs, is a general license to vigilantes and opportunists to resort to hegemonial intervention. (Brownlie 1973: 147–8.)

The problem with this criticism of vigilantes is that it implies that the only legitimate humanitarian intervention is one motivated purely by humanitarian considerations. To establish this requirement is too demanding, as few states will incur the risks and costs of humanitarian intervention for solely altruistic reasons. Given that motives will often be mixed, the key question becomes whether the non-humanitarian reasons for acting undermine the stated humanitarian purposes of the intervention.

Although India, Tanzania and Vietnam refrained from raising humanitarian claims to justify their use of force, each of these interventions produced a positive outcome despite being motivated primarily by security reasons. If a successful humanitarian outcome is the key test in judging the legitimacy of a humanitarian intervention, then India, Tanzania and Vietnam's actions would all count as legitimate humanitarian interventions. As it was, the society of states chose to name these actions as violations of UN Charter rules of sovereignty, non-intervention and non-use of force. The strong legal prohibition against humanitarian intervention in Charter law is also firmly embedded in customary international law, with General Assembly resolutions and the judgements of the ICJ providing little or no succour for those lawyers who claim that a legal right of humanitarian intervention is recognised in post-1945 international society.

Accepting the above interpretation of the law as reflecting the general view of states during the cold war raises the question as to what legitimacy we should attach to an international legal order that was silent in the face of massive human rights abuses by governments. If you ask those who were suffering under brutal tyrannies in East Pakistan, Cambodia or Uganda how they viewed the legitimacy of India, Vietnam and Tanzania's use of force, the answer would be very different from the meaning given to these actions by international society in the cold war. Even lawyers who are critical of legalising humanitarian intervention because of the fear that such a rule will be abused recognise that humanitarian intervention might be morally required in some cases. Writing in 1974, Thomas Franck and Nigel Rodley argued that humanitarian intervention 'belongs in the realm not of law but of moral choice, which nations, like individuals, must sometimes make' (Franck and Rodley 1974: 304), the implication being that states might decide in exceptional cases to privilege a moral duty to rescue strangers in danger over their legal obligations.

The argument that morality should be privileged over legality in cases of extreme human rights abuses is an unsatisfactory one for two reasons. In the first place, it underestimates the danger that such actions might set precedents that could lead to an erosion of international law. The choice then is better framed in terms of either accepting the moral consequences of non-intervention in the face of human wrongs, such as genocide, mass murder and ethnic cleansing, or risking the moral consequences that follow from states being perceived by others as setting themselves above the law. This leads into the second point, highlighted by Wil Verwey, which is that the very existence of this moral dilemma reflects the normative limitations of a system of international law which requires law-abiding states to avoid taking actions that are demanded by the requirements of common humanity (Verwey 1998: 200). Verwey argues that this fatally weakens international law because it 'would imply the recognition – no more, no less – that international law is incapable of ensuring respect for socially indispensable standards of morality' (Verwey 1998: 200).

Consequently, the challenge for those who want international law to serve as an instrument for the protection of human rights in the next century is to find ways of bridging the chasm that has opened up between the legal prohibition on the use of force and the need to enforce global humanitarian standards against genocide, mass murder and ethnic cleansing. At the same time, it is necessary to ensure that any new rules aimed at securing greater compliance with human rights norms do not serve to undermine the restraints against the use of force in international relations. A dialogue on these issues is long overdue in the society of states, but what has prevented such a conversation taking place is that particular states have been reluctant to act as norm entrepreneurs in this area. The next section takes up this challenge by asking how far NATO has advanced new normative claims in justifying its use of force in Kosovo.

NATO's Legal Justifications for its Use of Force in Kosovo

The most commonly invoked legal argument to justify NATO's use of force is that it was supported by Security Council Resolutions 1160, 1199 and 1203. Each of these resolutions was passed under Chapter VII of the Charter and demanded an end to the military action by Serbian forces and the Kosova Liberation Army. Resolution 1160 passed on 31 March determined that the situation in Kosovo constituted a threat to 'international peace and security' and condemned the excessive use of force by Serbian forces. This was

followed by Resolution 1199 on 23 September which restated the
Security Council's view that the threat to peace and security in the
region stemmed from the 'deterioration of the situation in Kosovo'. In
operative paragraphs one to four, it demanded that the FRY and the
Albanian leadership cease hostilities and take urgent steps to 'avert the
impending humanitarian catastrophe'. Resolution 1203 on 24 October
repeated the earlier resolutions on Kosovo with the Security Council
expressing its alarm at the 'impending humanitarian catastrophe'. This
resolution endorsed the agreement that was reached in October 1998
between Milošević and the US Envoy Richard Holbrooke which
averted the earlier threat of NATO air strikes. The British international
lawyer Marc Weller argues that this constituted an 'informal nod of
approval' by the Council for NATO's threat of force.[6] On the day that
NATO began its air strikes Russia convened an emergency meeting of
the Security Council to condemn the action. The Security Council had
at this time five NATO members on it and all these governments
justified their use of force in terms of Security Council Resolutions
1160, 1199 and 1203. In a deliberate move to invoke the key wording
in Resolutions 1199 and 1203, the five states claimed that NATO's
action was necessary to avoid a 'humanitarian catastrophe'.[7]

The fundamental weakness of NATO's legal defence is that
Resolutions 1160, 1199 and 1203 do not explicitly authorise the use
of force. The fact that the Security Council passed these three
resolutions under Chapter VII, and that each of these defined the
Kosovo crisis as a threat to peace and security in the region, does not
constitute a warrant for NATO enforcement action against the FRY.
Consequently, it is easy to see why critics argue that NATO's bombing
campaign is a violation of UN Charter law. Britain and the USA tried
to persuade Russia and China to support a stronger resolution
authorising NATO to use force, but it was clear that they would veto
any such draft resolution (Bellamy 1999: 30). Indeed, although Russia
voted in favour of Resolution 1199 (which secured 14 votes in total,
with China abstaining), both Russia and China issued statements before
the vote spelling out that the resolution should not be viewed as
endorsing the use of force. The Russian ambassador stated that 'No
measures of force and no sanctions at this stage were being introduced
by the Council [and that] ... Any use of force, especially unilateral,
would risk destabilizing the region.'[8] Similarly, the Chinese ambassador
declared that 'if the Security Council were to get involved in a dispute
without a request from the countries concerned ... it would create a
bad precedent and have wider negative implications'.[9]

Resolution 1199 requested the secretary-general to provide reports on how far the parties were complying with it, and on 5 October 1998 Kofi Annan presented a report which declared that he was 'outraged by reports of mass killings of civilians in Kosovo' (Youngs 1998: 13). The next day the Security Council met informally to discuss the secretary-general's report. Britain, which was president of the Council for October, took the lead in proposing a draft resolution specifically authorising 'all necessary means' to end the killings in Kosovo. However, this met with a Russian declaration that it would veto any such resolution.[10] A couple of days later, Russian embassies around the world issued a statement 'that the use of force against a sovereign state without due sanction of the UN Security Council would be an outright violation of the UN Charter, undermining the existing system of international relations'.[11]

The debate over Resolution 1203 did nothing to heal the widening rift that was opening up in the Security Council over the legality of NATO's threat to use force. This resolution was passed against the backdrop of Milošević's agreement to the deployment of OSCE monitors to verify the situation in Kosovo, which had been made possible by NATO's ultimatum on 12 October to use force. The resolution repeated the Council's earlier positions on Kosovo and was passed by 13 votes, with Russia and China abstaining. Despite growing Russian and Chinese sensitivities on the issue, the US ambassador stated that 'the threat of force was key to both achieving the OSCE and NATO agreements ... The NATO allies ... had the authority, the will, and the means to resolve the issue.'[12] Opposing this argument was Russia, which was determined to try and put the brakes on what it viewed as NATO's manipulation of Resolutions 1160 and 1199 to justify its threat to use force. To this end, the Russian ambassador reversed his previous position and argued that the Council did not have the authority to act under Chapter VII because 'it could not be agreed that the situation in Kosovo presented an international danger'. Moreover, the Russian ambassador continued that 'the use of force had been reflected in a draft and Russia would not condone that, it would abstain in the vote on the resolution'.[13] Russia was supported by China, which speaking after the vote indicated that there had been attempts during the negotiations to insert wording that 'authorized the use of force or the threat of the use of force' and that while this had been deleted from the final text, China had abstained owing to what it saw as a resolution 'to pressure the internal affairs of the Federal Republic of Yugoslavia'.[14]

It was not only Russia and China that were concerned by the argument being pressed by Britain and the USA on the legality of NATO's threat to use force. The then German Foreign Minister, Klaus Kinkel, was worried that the position taken by Russia and China in the Security Council made it very difficult to argue that existing Security Council resolutions authorised NATO's use of force (Guicherd 1999: 26–7). The question of German participation in any NATO air strikes against the FRY was an extremely sensitive one, given that the action would be outside the NATO area and in a region where there are bitter wartime memories of German intervention. The legal basis of any future NATO action was the subject of a debate in the German Bundestag in mid-October, and the outcome of this was that the Bundestag gave its approval for Germany to join in any air strikes (Simma 1999: 7). Despite his private reservations, Foreign Minister Kinkel argued that Resolution 1199 justified NATO's action. He stated: 'Under these unusual circumstances of the current crisis situation in Kosovo, as it is described in Resolution 1199 of the UN Security Council, the threat of and if need be the use of force by NATO is justified.'[15] However, he emphasised that Kosovo was a special case and that it should not be taken as a green light for future NATO actions outside the authority of the Security Council (Simma 1999: 7). Kinkel stated that 'NATO has not created a new legal instrument which could be the basis for a general licence for NATO to do interventions … NATO's decision must not become a precedent.'[16] In arguing that the action should not set a precedent, Kinkel was emphatic that there should be no more deviations from the rule of Security Council authorisation for the use of force. It is hard to resist the conclusion that Germany found itself in the difficult position of supporting an action on ethical grounds, knowing that this had, at best, a dubious basis in international law and, at worst, was illegal.

This position can be contrasted with the one taken by the incoming SPD-Green German government under Chancellor Gerhard Schroeder. Although the new government was uncomfortable with German participation in NATO air strikes without explicit UN authority, there was a greater willingness among ministers to advance new normative claims to justify NATO's position. Thus, the new defence minister, Rudolf Scharping, argued that international law should be developed so that massive human rights violations could be treated as a legitimate basis for the resort to force (Guicherd 1999: 27). Moreover, the future Minister of State in the German Foreign Ministry, Gunter Verheugen, addressed himself directly to the question of UN authorisation when he declared that a veto in the Security Council should not block states from intervening in cases where the level of killing offends against basic standards of common humanity:

> One can imagine a situation in which the level of violence became so great that every decent person would say something had to be done to end the killing. If Russia ... uses its Security Council veto one could say this was an abuse of the veto and argue the primacy of halting the slaughter is greater than formal respect of international law.[17]

What is important about the above statement is that there is no suggestion that there currently exists a legal right of humanitarian intervention outside of Security Council authorisation. Indeed, the minister recognises that he is proposing a course of action that is contrary to the formal strictures of international law. Pressing this argument within the Alliance, and the wider society of states, would cast the Schroeder government in the role of both a norm and legal entrepreneur, since it would be raising a new normative claim and arguing for a change of law to support this.

The Schroeder government's hesitation in claiming that NATO had the law on its side over Kosovo stands opposed to the British government's position that NATO's use of force had the authority of international law behind it. The Blair government denied that it was advancing new norms or creating new law; it accepted that its military intervention lacked express Security Council authorisation, but claimed to be enforcing existing Security Council resolutions. Moreover, the British government argued that there are precedents supporting the legality of NATO's action in Kosovo. The argument is that in exceptional cases states have a legal right to use force to avert a humanitarian disaster when this is in conformity with the purposes laid down by the Security Council even if there is no specific resolution authorising the action. This position was outlined by Baroness Symons, minister of state at the Foreign Office, in a written answer to Lord Kennet on 16 November 1998:

> There is no general doctrine of humanitarian necessity in international law. Cases have nevertheless arisen (as in northern Iraq in 1991) when, in the light of all the circumstances, a limited use of force was justifiable in support of purposes laid down by the Security Council but without the Council's express authorisation when that was the only means to avert an

immediate and overwhelming humanitarian catastrophe. Such cases would in the nature of things be exceptional and would depend on an objective assessment of the factual circumstances at the time and on the terms of relevant decisions of the Security Council bearing on the situation in question.[18]

Some two months before the air strikes began, Foreign Office Minister Tony Lloyd was questioned before the House of Commons Foreign Affairs Select Committee on this legal justification. In response to questions from Ted Rowlands and Diane Abbott as to whether there was a legal right for NATO to take action given the divisions within the Security Council over how to respond to the humanitarian crisis in Kosovo, the minister replied: 'Within those terms yes. International law certainly gives the legal base in the way that I have described ... we believed at that time [October 1998] that the humanitarian crisis was such as to warrant that intervention'.[19]

The British government's contention that there is a secure 'legal base' for NATO's action in customary international law is strongly supported by the British international lawyer Christopher Greenwood, who contends that:

> In recent years, states have come, perhaps reluctantly, to accept that there is a right of humanitarian intervention when a government – or the factions in a civil war – create a human tragedy of such magnitude that it constitutes a threat to international peace. In such a case, if the Security Council does not take military action, then other states have a right to do so. It is from this state practice that the right of humanitarian intervention on which NATO now relies has emerged. Those who contest that right are forced to conclude that even though international law outlaws what the Yugoslav Government is doing ... if the Security Council cannot act, the rest of the world has to stand aside. That is not what international law requires at the end of the century (Greenwood 1999).[20]

The Security Council is the formal law-enforcement body in international society, but if it fails to act to stop a humanitarian catastrophe, states have a legal right (but not necessarily a duty) to take the enforcement of humanitarian law into their own hands. This extends to the international realm the classic argument for vigilante action in domestic society. NATO would have preferred to act as a posse with the full authority of the Security Council behind it, but as

Brown puts it, the choice was 'not posse or vigilantes, but vigilantes or nothing' (Brown 1999: 13).

The above interpretation of NATO action is superficially attractive, and it suits Britain and the USA to present their actions as in conformity with current international law. However, the vigilante defence breaks down because some Alliance governments, especially Britain, are exaggerating how far there is a legal right of humanitarian intervention without Security Council authority. Whatever the British government might say to the contrary, its justification for NATO's use of force in Kosovo leads to the conclusion that it is not so much taking existing law into its own hands as establishing a normative precedent that might *become* the basis of new law.

The key case that Baroness Symons invoked in defence of the argument that there is a legal right to use force without express Security Council authorisation was the allied intervention in northern Iraq to create 'safe havens' for the Kurds in April 1991. The Security Council determined in Resolution 688 that the transboundary consequences of Iraq's aggression against the Kurds constituted a threat to 'international peace and security'. However, the resolution was not passed under Chapter VII and there was no question of the Council having authorised western governments to use force to protect the Kurds. Consequently, it might be argued that Allied action in setting up the northern no-fly zone and safe havens exceeded the limits of permissible action under Resolution 688. Yet no state on the Security Council challenged western military intervention as a breach of Iraqi sovereignty and this might be read as a tacit legitimation of western action.

Nevertheless, to claim as Baroness Symons did in her written answer to Lord Kennet, that the international response to Allied intervention in northern Iraq supports a new custom of intervention without explicit Council authorisation is highly problematic for three reasons. First, no western state justified its action in these terms, preferring to rely instead on the contention that Resolution 688 provided sufficient authorisation for the military action. Consequently, it cannot be known whether other governments would have responded differently had Allied governments invoked the claim that they were acting without the authority of a specific Security Council resolution. Second, since customary international law requires both state practice and *opinio juris*, there is the question as to whether to read the silence that greeted the Allied actions as recognition that such actions are permitted by international law. Lastly, and perhaps most importantly, the humanitarian justification for the intervention in northern Iraq was consistent with the operations that Allied forces undertook on the ground. Had the operation to rescue the Kurds required the use of force against Iraqi forces, or even an air bombardment of Iraqi civilian targets, it is likely that there would have been much greater opposition in the Security Council to what would have been interpreted as a clear breach of Iraq's territorial integrity under Article 2 (4) of the UN Charter.

Although NATO governments have tried to hide behind the fig-leaf supplied by Resolutions 1160, 1199 and 1203, rather than explicitly argue for a new norm that would recognise exceptions to Security Council authorisation, the international response to NATO's action has divided the society of states into those who interpret the action as a dangerous breach of the law and those who cautiously welcome this normative development.

The International Response to NATO's Action

Some two days after the NATO bombing began, Russia tabled with India and Belarus a draft resolution condemning NATO's action as a breach of Articles 2 (4), 24 and 53 of the UN Charter and demanding a cessation of hostilities.[21] States routinely invoke Article 2 (4) when they want to criticise the use of force by other states, but the claim that NATO was violating Articles 24 and 53 took the debate on the legitimate use of force into new territory. Article 24 refers to the primary responsibility of the Security Council for the maintenance of international peace and security, with UN member states agreeing that the Security Council should act 'on their behalf' in carrying out this function. Under Article 53 of the Charter, the Security Council is empowered to 'utilise ... regional arrangements or agencies for enforcement action', but the Charter is explicit that this can only take place with authorisation by the Security Council. Consequently, NATO is charged with usurping the Security Council's primary responsibility, with the Russian ambassador arguing that what was 'in the balance now was law and lawlessness; of either reaffirming the commitments of one's people to the United Nations Charter, or tolerating a situation where gross force was the norm'.[22] Ukraine and Belarus repeated the Russian line that NATO's actions were illegal, and this position was strongly supported by China which opposed NATO's action as a blatant violation of the principles of the Charter, as well as international law, and challenging the Council's authority. The Indian representative stated 'that NATO believed itself to be above the law, and that was deeply uncomfortable'.[23] Indeed, India challenged the legitimacy of NATO's action by pointing out that representatives of half of humanity (Russia, India and China) had opposed NATO's action as a flagrant breach of the Charter.[24]

Vigilantes claim to enforce the law in the absence of action by legally constituted law-enforcement agencies, but what is apparent from the debate in the Security Council is that NATO's interpretation of the law is strongly contested by some of the most powerful states. There are three interpretations of the opposition expressed in the Council to NATO's action. The first is that these states are good pluralists in international society terms who are worried that NATO's action sets a dangerous precedent for the rule of law in international relations. The concern is that other states, or groups of states, might use force without express Security Council authorisation, invoking the very arguments that NATO used to justify its action in Kosovo. This might not be a worry if there was consensus on the normative standards that should govern a rule permitting humanitarian intervention, but for pluralists it is exactly this lack of consensus which makes this kind of intervention such a threat to international order. Thus, states such as Russia, China and India that have internalised pluralist norms treat NATO's action as a dangerous breach of the rules that justifies moral condemnation.

There is a less charitable interpretation, however, of the positions taken by Russia, China and India. The argument is that they are using the language of the UN Charter to mask their real concern, which is that NATO's action could have unpredictable consequences for their own restive minorities in Chechyna,[25] Tibet and Kashmir. The Russian and Chinese veto in the Security Council enables these states to shield their own human rights abuses, and those of their friends, from international action. Yet, in acting outside the formal rules of the UN Charter, NATO has placed Russia and China on notice that it will not let their vetoes stand in the way of armed intervention in cases where there are massive violations of human rights.

The arguments advanced by Russia, China, India, Belarus and Ukraine against NATO's action are familiar ones that have been voiced in all previous cases where a humanitarian claim might have been raised in defence of an action. However, in this case, there was a twist in the tail. First, humanitarian claims were being explicitly invoked to justify the use of force and, second, 12 members of the Security Council voted against the Russian resolution tabled against NATO's action with only Russia, China and Namibia supporting it.

The five NATO members on the Council rejected the charge that they were acting outside the UN Charter, justifying their actions as being in conformity with existing resolutions and necessary to prevent a humanitarian catastrophe. It is noteworthy that no NATO member explicitly argued that the failure of the Security Council to act bestowed upon NATO a legal right of humanitarian intervention. Of the seven non-permanent members who rejected the draft resolution, four chose to make statements. Malaysia and Bahrain reiterated the standard NATO argument that the humanitarian catastrophe taking place inside Kosovo justified NATO's action, but Slovenia and Argentina made important contributions to the debate.

Slovenia admitted that it would have preferred direct Council authorisation, but expressed its regret 'that not all permanent members of the Council were willing to act in accordance with their special responsibility for international peace and security'.[26] This was clearly directed at Russia and China's refusal to give NATO authorisation to use force, but it also represented a response to the charge that NATO was acting contrary to Article 24 of the UN Charter. The Slovenian ambassador considered that 'Council members had to think hard about what needed to be done to ensure the Council's authority and make its primary responsibility as real as the Charter required.'[27] It was Russia and China who, by failing to act responsibly, were preventing the Security Council from exercising its 'primary responsibility for the maintenance of international peace and security' under Article 24. Argentina stated that its rejection of the draft resolution was based on contributing to efforts to stop the massive violations of human rights in Kosovo. Indeed, the Argentinean ambassador went further, arguing that the obligation to protect human rights and 'fulfil the legal norms of international humanitarian law ... was the obligation of all and must not be debated'.[28] The implication was that in exceptional circumstances such as those prevailing in Kosovo, states have a right to use force to put an end to human rights violations.

The Security Council debate on 26 March is the first time in the UN's history that members have legitimated the use of force against another sovereign state on humanitarian grounds. Rather than naming NATO's action as a breach of the rules of sovereignty, non-intervention and non-use of force, the majority of members chose to interpret it as a legitimate enforcement action in defence of the humanitarian purposes laid down by the Security Council. Moreover, with the exception of a small vocal minority, wider international society either tacitly accepted or strongly supported NATO's action. Realists would argue that the powerful are always able to create a legitimacy convenient to themselves, and this criticism was expressed by Cuba when it claimed that the 'shameful' 12 votes cast in support of NATO's action showed the 'Council going along with actions of international delinquency by the United States and its allies'.[29] An alternative reading of this historic vote in the Security Council is that NATO, as a reluctant norm entrepreneur, has begun a process of norm creation that is leading the society of states to legitimise the use of force in defence of global humanitarian values. The question that has to be addressed in the aftermath of the Kosovo case is whether this process should be solely dependent upon explicit Security Council authorisation, left to develop out of *ad hoc* responses to specific situations, or placed under specific norms that determine the conditions under which the Security Council can be bypassed.

Conclusions

In his speech given to the Economic Club of Chicago on 22 April 1999, Prime Minister Blair argued that the non-intervention principle 'must be qualified in important respects' when massive human rights violations are taking place (Blair 1999: 8). At the same time, he argued that 'new rules' restricting sovereign prerogatives would only work if the Security Council avoided the deadlock that paralysed it during the cold war. Blair's vision of the principles underpinning the 'doctrine of international community' did not go as far as advancing the case for a new rule that would exempt states from requiring Security Council authorisation in exceptional cases of human suffering. Instead, he left it open as to what Britain and the Alliance would do if faced with a future situation where a Russian and Chinese veto was blocking a humanitarian rescue mission.

The experience of the 1990s suggests that the Security Council is too weak to uphold the civilised values of the international community. In 1991, it was divided over the use of force to protect the Kurds; at the end of the decade, it was unable to issue NATO with a warrant for its threat and use of force in Kosovo. Given the volatile domestic situation in Russia, and the heightened sensitivity of Russia and China to actions that erode the sovereignty rule, it is highly unlikely that the permanent members of the Security Council will become a humanitarian coalition of the willing in future cases of gross human rights abuses.

In the case of Kosovo, even without explicit Security Council authorisation, NATO states were able to claim that they were enforcing agreed Security Council resolutions. This context enabled NATO to argue that it was enforcing existing law rather than creating new law, but this vigilante defence is unlikely to be available to the Alliance in future situations involving human rights violations by a sovereign government. Having watched NATO argue that the very adoption of a resolution under Chapter VII provides a legal basis for military action in Kosovo, Russia and China will be much more cautious about passing such resolutions in future cases. This raises the fascinating counterfactual question as to how NATO would have legitimised its action in Kosovo in the absence of Resolutions 1160, 1199 and 1203. Would NATO have been inhibited from acting or would the search for legality have compelled governments to argue that there is a legal right of humanitarian intervention in cases of supreme humanitarian emergency? If NATO governments had acted as legal entrepreneurs, then it would have been the first time in post-1945 international society that a group of states had explicitly justified their use of force in terms of the legal doctrine of humanitarian intervention.

Yet, even if NATO governments had explicitly invoked customary law to support their use of force, it is unlikely that this would have produced a different response in the society of states. The overwhelming vote against the Russian resolution condemning NATO's action in the Security Council, and the absence of any criticism from the majority of southern states, suggests that a new norm is being created that restricts sovereign rights in cases of gross human rights abuses. The dominant political and economic position of the west clearly goes some way to explaining why so few states opposed NATO's action, indicating that success as a norm entrepreneur depends upon the ability to mobilise power. However, an equally significant factor in changing the normative boundaries of legitimate humanitarian intervention is the spread of democratic values. For example, the strong support that Argentina expressed for NATO's action in the Security Council has to be located in its identity as a democratic state, confirming the constructivist contention that states that identify with human rights values domestically will be more inclined to defend them internationally (Finnemore and Sikkink 1998: 902).

The emergence of a new norm of humanitarian intervention is strongly opposed by Russia, China and India. This raises the question of how many states have to validate a new norm before it can be said to have acquired the status of a new customary law? What if some of the objectors to a new rule are among the most powerful states in the world? Michael Byers (1999: 159) makes the point that where there is only one case of past practice in support of a new rule, states can easily nullify it by acting against it in future instances. Given the record of state practice against a rule of humanitarian intervention, it will require additional cases to the Kosovo one where state practice and *opinio juris* support a new rule before a judgement can be made as to how far there has been a lasting change in the legitimacy of humanitarian intervention in the society of states.

Having set the precedent in the case of Kosovo for acting outside express Security Council authorisation, there is the worry that other states might choose to do the same. At the same time, there is the concern that NATO's bypassing of the Russian and Chinese veto might weaken the authority of the Security Council. With regard to the latter, the widespread support for NATO's action suggests that there is also a recognition that the power of the veto brings with it responsibilities to uphold minimal standards of humanity. If the words 'We the Peoples', in the Preamble of the UN Charter, have meaning, then it has to be asked why Russia and China should have a veto over the actions of an alliance comprised of 19 democratically elected sovereign states that are enforcing human rights norms.

The question of whether NATO's action sets a dangerous precedent for other states to use force outside the authority of the Security Council is a difficult one, and this was the argument mobilised against NATO by Russia, China and India. However, rather than conclude that a new rule legitimising humanitarian intervention is too dangerous a threat to international order, the best response is to follow Henry Shue's suggestion that all decisions on humanitarian intervention be subject to independent review by the society of states (Shue 1998: 71–7). States would have to make the case that all peaceful means of intervention had been exhausted, that they had only acted because the Security Council had been paralysed by the threat or use of a Russian or Chinese veto, and that their use of force was justified to prevent or stop mass atrocities. If these justifications were judged unconvincing by the Security Council and the General Assembly, then the society of states would have the power of shaming and even sanctioning at its disposal (Shue 1998: 76). While critics might argue that having to answer before the court of world public opinion is a weak defence against states determined to exploit a rule of humanitarian intervention for their own selfish purposes, an admixture of moral censure and economic sanctions might at least exercise a significant deterrent effect.

A process of independent review would not only serve to constrain states from abusing a rule of humanitarian intervention, it would also legitimise intervention to stop massive human rights abuses. By building up a series of judgements that established the norms of legitimate action, states would have greater assurance that humanitarian intervention would be welcomed by the society of states. Indeed, this collective legitimation might take the form of political, economic and military support for the intervening state, thereby encouraging governments to incur the costs and risks of humanitarian intervention. However, creating a new norm that enables humanitarian intervention is no guarantee that it will take place in cases where it is urgently required (Shue 1998: 76).

The positive interpretation of NATO's action in Kosovo is that the moral claims raised in defence of Kosovo Albanians will make it very difficult for the Alliance to look on with indifference the next time gross human rights abuses occur in Europe or elsewhere. The problem with this argument is that it overlooks the fact that the humanitarian impulse to act in Kosovo was joined by a recognition that NATO had important security interests at stake in the region. This combination of humanitarian emergency and hard-headed security interests is unlikely to confront the Alliance outside of a European context, and this suggests that the west will be as selective in its interventions to stop human rights abuses in the future as it has been in the past. Yet since the problem of selectivity fuels the belief held by China and Russia that humanitarian claims are always a cover for the pursuit of western interests (Lloyd 1999: 8–9), it is an issue that will have to be addressed if a new norm of humanitarian intervention is to secure lasting legitimacy in the society of states.

NOTES

1. For a detailed analysis of cold-war and post-cold-war cases of humanitarian intervention, see Wheeler (forthcoming).
2. Bull contrasted the solidarist conception with a pluralist one in which consensus is restricted to upholding the rules of sovereignty, non-intervention and non-use of force. See Bull (1966).
3. The idea of the posse is developed by Brown (1999: 11–12). The idea of states as 'norm entrepreneurs' was first developed by Martha Finnemore and Kathryn Sikkink (1998).
4. In the 1990s, the Security Council began to exercise its Chapter VII powers to respond to humanitarian emergencies. By defining these crises as threats to 'international peace and security' under Article 39 of the UN Charter, the Security Council provided a warrant for US, French and NATO interventions in Somalia, Rwanda and Bosnia-Herzegovina respectively. This is in stark contrast to the cold-war

context where there was no consensus in the Council to define human rights violations or even their transboundary consequences as threats to 'international peace and security'.

5. Fernando Teson argues that the muted response to Tanzania's intervention in Uganda indicates that there are precedents supporting the legality of humanitarian intervention during the cold war. However, there are two problems with this claim: first, President Nyerere never sought to defend his action in these terms, even when confronted with criticism from Sudan and Nigeria at the OAU Summit in Monrovia in July 1979; and, second, with the exception of the new government installed by Tanzanian arms in Kampala, no member of international society justified the action on legal grounds. Consequently, the Tanzanian case does not support the claim that there is a customary rule of humanitarian intervention because the practice lacked the critical requirement of *opinio juris*.

6. *The Guardian*, Allies argue humanitarian case, 25 March 1999.
7. United Nations Security Council Press Release SC/6657, 24 March 1999, p.9.
8. United Nations Security Council Press Release SC/6577, 23 September 1999, p.8.
9. Ibid., pp.8–9.
10. *Electronic Telegraph*, Britain and US may have to go it alone, 8 October 1998. Russian Foreign Minister, Igor Ivanov, told Interfax news agency that 'Russia would definitely use its right of veto'. See *Electronic Telegraph*, 7 October 1998.
11. *Electronic Telegraph*, Britain and US may have to go it alone, 8 October 1998.
12. United Nations Security Council Press Release SC/6588, 24 October 1999, p.14.
13. Ibid., p.13.
14. Ibid., p.14.
15. Deutscher Bundestag, Plenarprotokoll 13/248 vom 16.10.1998, p.21, 329.
16. Ibid.
17. *Electronic Telegraph*, Germany will send jets to Kosovo, 1 October 1998.
18. The use of the language of averting 'an immediate and overwhelming humanitarian catastrophe' was a deliberate move to make an explicit link to the Security Council's demands in Resolutions 1199 and 1203. See Baroness Symons of Vernham Dean, written answer to Lord Kennet, Hansard, 16 November 1998, Col.WA 140.
19. House of Commons Minute of Evidence taken before the Foreign Affairs Committee, 26 January 1999, p.35
20. It is worth noting that Christopher Greenwood was part of Britain's legal team which appeared before the International Court of Justice in the case concerning the legality of NATO's use of force, 10 May 1999.
21. United Nations Security Council Press Release SC/6659, 26 March 1999, p.3.
22. Ibid., p.6
23. Ibid., p.13
24. Ibid.
25. In addition to this reason, a key factor behind Russia's opposition to NATO's action was the fear that the old adversary was expanding its sphere of influence in ways that threatened Russian interests. This view was espoused by Boris Yeltsin during the crisis when the Russian president commented, 'Bill Clinton wants to win ... He hopes Milošević will capitulate, give up the whole of Yugoslavia, make it America's protectorate.' Quoted in Reuters, 'NATO: flow of Kosovar refugees mysteriously slows to a trickle', 20 April 1999.
26. United Nations Security Council Press Release SC/6659, 26 March 1999, p.4
27. Ibid.
28. Ibid., pp.7–8.
29. The Cuban ambassador declared that 'Never before had the unipolar order imposed by the United States been so obvious ... When the Council did not yield to unipolar might, then what had been seen was that the super-Power acted on its own.' Ibid., p.11.

REFERENCES

Arend, A. C. and Beck, R. J. 1993, *International Law and the Use of Force: Beyond the UN Charter Paradigm.* London, Routledge.
Bellamy, A.J. 1999. Is Nato's bombing of Serbia actually legal? *Interstate*, 54, pp.29–32.
Blair, T. 1999. Speech to the Economic Club of Chicago, 22 April 1999. www.fco.gov.uk.
Brown, C. 1992, *International Relations Theory: New Normative Approaches.* Hemel Hempstead: Harvester Wheatsheaf.
—— 1999. The artificial person of international society. Unpublished Paper.
Brownlie, I., 1973. Thoughts on kind-hearted gunmen. In *Humanitarian Intervention and the United Nations*, ed. Lillich, R.B. Charlottesville, University Press of Virginia.
Bull, H., 1966. The Grotian conception of international society. In *Diplomatic Investigations*, ed. Wight, M. and Butterfield, H. London, Allen & Unwin.
—— 1984. Conclusion. In *Intervention in World Politics*, ed. Bull, H. Oxford, Clarendon.
Byers, M. 1999, *Custom, Power and the Power of Rules.* Cambridge: Cambridge University Press.
Finnemore, M. and Sikkink, K. 1998. International norm dynamics and political change. *International Organization*, Vol.52, No.4, pp.887–917.
Franck, T. and Rodley, N. 1974. After Bangladesh: the law of humanitarian intervention by force. *American Journal of International Law*, Vol.67, No.2, pp.275–305.
Frost, M. 1996, *Ethics in International Relations.* Cambridge: Cambridge University Press.
Greenwood, C. 1999. Yes, but is the war legal? *The Observer*, 28 March 1999.
Guicherd, C. 1999. International law and the war in Kosovo. *Survival*, Vol.41, No.2, pp.19–33.
Lloyd, J. 1999. Kosovo: a rich and comfortable war. *New Statesman*, June 1999.
Shue, H., 1998. Let whatever is smouldering erupt? Conditional sovereignty, reviewable intervention, and Rwanda 1994. In *Between Sovereignty and Global Governance: The United Nations, the State and Civil Society*, eds. Paolini, A.J., Jarvis, A.P. and Reus-Smit, C. London, Macmillan.
Simma, B. 1999, *NATO, the UN and the Use of Force: Legal Aspects.* http://www.ejil.org/journal/Vol10/No1/ab1-2-html.
Teson, F.R. 1988, *Humanitarian Intervention: An Inquiry into Law and Morality.* Dobbs Ferry (NY): Transnational Publishers Inc.
Verwey, W.D., 1998. Humanitarian intervention in the 1990s and beyond. In *World Orders in the Making: Humanitarian Intervention and Beyond*, ed. Pieterse, J.N. London, Macmillan.
Wheeler, N.J. 2000, *Saving Strangers: Humanitarian Intervention in International Society.* Oxford: Oxford University Press.
Youngs, T. 1998. *Kosovo: The Diplomatic and Military Options.* Research Paper 98/93, House of Commons Library, 27 October 1998.

Abstracts

Derrida and the Heidegger Controversy: Global Friendship Against Racism
MARK BEVIR

This essay explores the ethical import of deconstruction through a reading of Derrida on Heidegger. In *Of Spirit*, Derrida traces through Heidegger's writings the interplay of 'spirit' and spirit. Spirit denotes an involvement with the question of Being, and in thus pointing toward a positive content, it embodies a metaphysical gesture in which a spiritual mission becomes the human essence. In Heidegger's entanglement with National Socialism, he tied this spiritual mission to German self-assertion. 'Spirit' is a concept under erasure that calls our attention to the absent Other. It reminds us of an ethical responsibility that is prior to ontology; it sets up a 'cosmopolitanism' that precedes all particular identifications and so avoids spiritual racism. Derridean 'cosmopolitanism' differs importantly from liberal universalism. From a Derridean perspective, liberal universalism remains insufficiently attuned to the Other; it retains a metaphysical gesture, and so an imperialistic and exclusionary tendency, akin to that found in Heidegger.

Cosmopolitanism, World Citizenship and Global Civil Society
CHRIS BROWN

The notion that an emergent 'global civil society' exists has become a commonplace of recent globalist literature; the burden of this essay is that this terminology is misleading. Properly understood, 'civil society' requires an effective state, while global civil society is characteristically seen as a substitute for such a political order. Furthermore, it may be doubted that the mind-set required to make a civil society work actually exists in the world today. What is at stake here is not simply an academic mislabelling; serious consequences follow from the systematic undervaluing of political reform that the 'global civil society' usage encourages.

Human Rights, Compatibility and Diverse Cultures
SIMON CANEY

Do global norms, such as human rights, conflict with non-western cultures? If so, does it matter? This paper examines the issues surrounding the relationship between human rights and non-western ethical traditions. It has three aims. First, it provides an account of the various ways in which ethical traditions may relate to human rights, challenging the binary assumption that ethical traditions either explicitly affirm human rights or repudiate them. Second, it explores the moral significance of the relationship between human rights and ethical traditions, arguing that harmony between human rights and ethical traditions has prima-facie value. Lastly, it moves from theoretical discussions to an examination of one specific non-western ethical tradition, Theravada Buddhism. The latter, it is argued, does not conflict with human rights and represents an interesting counter-example to the conventional wisdom that non-western ethical traditions are hostile to human rights.

The Pendulum Theory of Individual, Communal and Minority Rights
TOM HADDEN

There are a number of prevalent misconceptions among political theorists about the nature of human rights: that they can only be recognised for human beings as individuals, that they are absolute and unchanging, and that they are of equal status. Even a brief study of the development of human rights law shows that, in reality, the recognition of human rights, especially those concerning communal and minority rights, has varied over time, swinging backward and forward between the recognition and denial of group rights in line with prevailing political ideologies. Political theorists (and human rights lawyers) need to recognise and learn to manage these swings of the rights pendulum, rather than attempt to use human rights as the foundation for grand theories of global citizenship.

The Question of Self-Determination and its Implications for Normative International Theory
KIMBERLY HUTCHINGS

This article looks critically at the way in which the ideal of self-determination operates in a range of normative debates about individual and collective rights within the international arena. It argues that mainstream cosmopolitan and communitarian approaches to questions of self-determination are fundamentally flawed by their reliance both on an idealised ontology of mutually exclusive 'selves' (individual or collective) and on an unsustainable position of epistemological privilege on the part of the normative theorist. The article goes on to explore some alternative approaches to thinking about the issue of self-determination. It concludes that, in spite of a variety of shortcomings, the work of critical, post-modernist and feminist theorists does offer a more satisfactory way forward for normative theorising about issues of self-determination than more orthodox ethical approaches.

Human Rights and Diverse Cultures: Continuity or Discontinuity?
PETER JONES

Diversity of belief and value is a conspicuous feature of the human condition. A theory of human rights, if it is to be plausible and appealing, must accommodate that diversity in some considerable measure. This article examines two strategies that we might pursue in trying to reconcile human rights with human diversity: the strategies of continuity and discontinuity. A 'continuous' strategy tries to uncover a core of rights acknowledged by all cultures and systems of belief, so that we can establish a continuity of commitment from those diverse cultures and systems of belief to a common set of human rights. A 'discontinuous' strategy, by contrast, aims to reconcile the theory of human rights with a variety of cultures and beliefs by giving it a foundation and a purpose that is categorically different from, and independent of, those cultures and beliefs. The article casts doubt on the continuous strategy and defends the discontinuous strategy, but also acknowledges that there are some sorts of value conflict upon which a theory of human rights must take a stand rather than aspire to be a 'second-level' regulator.

Humanitarian Vigilantes or Legal Entrepreneurs: Enforcing Human Rights in International Society
NICHOLAS J. WHEELER

This article examines the legitimacy and legality of NATO's military intervention in Kosovo in March 1999. It examines how far this case supports a new norm of humanitarian intervention in international society. Here, it draws upon three models for thinking about the question of collective legitimation: the posse, the vigilante and the norm entrepreneur. I argue that the latter two models are most relevant to understanding NATO's action. Western governments tried to justify their actions as upholding the authority of existing Security Council resolutions, but, I show the weaknesses of this claim and maintain that NATO is better seen as advancing a new norm of humanitarian intervention in the society of states. The article then assesses how far these claims were legitimated and I contend that this case marks a significant change in the normative boundaries of legitimate intervention. Nevertheless, I conclude by showing how the legitimacy of humanitarian intervention is contested by major states in international society, and argue that there will have to be more cases supporting this practice before it can be said to have acquired the status of a new rule of customary international law.

Notes on Contributors

Mark Bevir is an Assistant Professor in the Department of Political Science at the University of California, Berkeley. His research and writing has focused on modern political thought, especially British socialism, and the philosophy of history. He is the author of *The Logic of the History of Ideas* (Cambridge University Press, 1999).

Chris Brown is the author of *International Relations Theory: New Normative Approaches* (Harvester Wheatsheaf, 1992), *Understanding International Relations* (Macmillan, 1997) and of some two dozen articles and chapters on international political theory. He is currently working on a book on cultural diversity and international political theory. He is Professor of International Relations at the LSE and the President and immediate past Chair of the British International Studies Association.

Simon Caney teaches political philosophy at the University of Newcastle. He is the co-editor, with Peter Jones and David George, of *National Rights, International Obligations* (Westview, 1996). He has also published articles in philosophy, politics and law journals on contemporary liberal political philosophy and issues surrounding global ethics. He is currently working on a book entitled *Global Political Theory*.

Tom Hadden is a part-time Professor of Law at Queen's University, Belfast, where he teaches in the postgraduate human rights programme. He has written extensively with Professor Kevin Boyle of the University of Essex on the application of human rights principles to Northern Ireland and other areas of conflict and was the founding editor of *Fortnight: an Independent Review for Northern Ireland.* He has also worked on issues of corporate governance and other politico-legal topics in company law. He has recently been appointed as a part-time Commissioner of the new Northern Ireland Human Rights Commission.

Kimberly Hutchings is Senior Lecturer in Politics at the University of Edinburgh. She has published widely in the field of post-Kantian social and political theory, including international political theory. She is the author of *Kant, Critique and Politics* (Routledge, 1996); *Cosmopolitan Citizenship* (edited with Roland Dannreuther, Macmillan, 1999); and *International Political Theory: Re-Thinking Ethics in a Global Era* (Sage, 1999). She is currently working on a book, *Hegel and Feminist Philosophy* (Polity, forthcoming).

Peter Jones is Professor of Political Philosophy at the University of Newcastle. He has written on a variety of subjects in contemporary political philosophy, including democracy, freedom, toleration, welfare policy, human rights, group rights, and international justice. His recent work has focused on the question of how we should provide for diversities of belief and value, both globally and within individual societies. He is the author of *Rights* (Macmillan, 1994) and the editor, with Simon Caney and David George, of *National Rights, International Obligations* (Westview, 1996).

Nicholas J. Wheeler is a Senior Lecturer in International Politics at the University of Wales, Aberystwyth. He has written widely on human rights and humanitarian intervention and is the author of *Saving Strangers: Humanitarian Intervention in International Society* (Oxford University Press, 2000).

Index

Index

Abbott, Diane 152
abortion 46–8, 114, 115
Africa 17, 23
alienation 14–15
alterity 126, 128, 131, 132, 134, 135
  see also other
American Declaration of Independence 78, 82
Amnesty International 140
An-Na'im, Abdullahi 49, 54, 58, 65, 71
Annan, Kofi 149
arbitration: international 16–17
Argentina 156, 158
Aristotle 7, 55
Augustine, Saint 57
Aurelius, Marcus 7, 8
autonomy 14, 69, 99, 103, 110, 111, 133
  see also self-determination: individual

Bahrain 156
Bangladesh 17
  see also East Pakistan
Barber, Benjamin 19
Being 122–3, 124, 125, 126, 127, 129–30
Belarus 154
Belief: freedom of 46
Bell, Daniel 54, 65
Bevir, Mark 4
Blair, Tony 141, 151, 157
Bosnia 141
Britain 148, 149, 150, 151–2, 153, 157
  see also United Kingdom
Brown, Chris 2, 140, 141, 153
Brownlie, Ian 145
Buchanan, Allen 69
Buddhism: 55

and human rights 66–70
  Theravada 3, 52, 64–6, 69
Bull, Hedley 140, 144
Burma 64
Byers, Michael 159

Cambodia 64, 144, 146
Canada 18, 94
Caney, Simon 3
Canovan, Margaret 97–8, 105
Cassesse, Antonio 71
Chan, Joseph 54
Chechnya 155
China 148, 149–50, 154, 155, 156, 157, 158, 160
Christianity 32, 55
circumcision: female 113, 114, 115
citizenship 2, 8–9, 10, 24, 106, 111
civil society: 10, 11, 18, 20, 21
  and state 12–13, 22
  emergence of 13–15
  global 2, 9–11, 15–18, 19, 21–3, 24
  North Atlantic 10, 18–19, 20
CNN 17
Cold War 6, 142, 146
communitarianism 92, 101–4, 107, 108, 109, 112, 113, 116
Confucianism 54, 55, 61, 65
consensus: overlapping 34–5, 37, 41, 54
  see also human rights: consensual approach
continuity *see* human rights: consensual approach
contractarianism 92–3, 94, 96
  see also statism: liberal
contract: social 72

Lightning Source UK Ltd.
Milton Keynes UK
27 October 2009

145481UK00001B/2/A